T0156516

TOP SECRETS FOR BUILDING A BETTER YOU

New Strategies and Techniques for Having a More Fulfilling Life

by Gini Graham Scott, PhD

Author of *Want It, See It, Get It!, Enjoy! 101 Little Ways to Add Fun to Your Work Everyday, Playing the Lying Game, 30 Days to a More Powerful Memory,* and *50+ Other Books*

iUniverse, Inc.
New York   Bloomington

iUniverse books may be ordered through booksellers or by contacting:

iUniverse
1663 Liberty Drive
Bloomington, IN 47403
www.iuniverse.com
1-800-Authors (1-800-288-4677)

ISBN: 978-1-4502-1431-5 (sc)

Library of Congress Control Number: 2010903765

Printed in the United States of America

iUniverse rev. date: 03/09/2010

Table of Contents

Overview

TOP SECRETS BUILDING A BETTER YOU developed out of a radio program I did from September 2009 to February 2010 called CHANGEMAKERS through HealthyLife.Net Radio, which is syndicated to 400,000 plus listeners, primarily throughout the U.S. The program focused on change – in society and in oneself. As part of this program, which explored new ventures, discoveries, social trends, explorations in human consciousness, and more provided some tips and techniques for changing and improving yourself.

TOP SECRETS FOR BUILDING A BETTER YOU features these tips and techniques and builds upon ideas for personal and professional development described in some of my other books, including techniques for visualizing and getting what you want in life -- *WANT IT, SEE IT, GET IT! VISUALIZE YOUR WAY TO SUCCESS; MIND POWER: PICTURE YOUR WAY TO SUCCESS; THE EMPOWERED MIND: HOW TO HARNESS THE CREATIVE FORCE WITHIN YOU; PLAYING THE LYING GAME; 30 DAYS TO A MORE POWERFUL MEMORY; RESOLVING CONFLICT*; and many others.

In some of the chapters, the initial discussion and tips for making changes in one's life is followed by a guided visualization, which I created for the first five radio shows. Once you have the general idea, you can create your own visualizations.

About the Author

Gini Graham Scott is the author of over 50 books with major publishers, a screenplay writer and indy film producer, and a radio host on Changemakers Radio.

As a prolific and diverse writer for over 25 years, Gini Graham Scott has written both her own books and books for clients. Her recent books focus on work issues, creativity, management, marketing, resolving conflict, and change. She is a speaker, workshop/seminar leader, and an organizational consultant to business, government and non-profit organizations. She has spoken to top executives, managers, professionals, and the general public.

Her latest books are PLAYING THE LYING GAME, WANT IT, SEE IT, GET IT! VISUALIZE YOUR WAY TO SUCCESS and ENJOY! 101 LITTLE WAYS TO ADD FUN TO YOUR WORK EVERYDAY. Her column on relationships in work and business has been in a dozen papers, including the Oakland Tribune and THE L.A. Downtown News. It was expanded into a book published as A SURVIVAL GUIDE FOR WORKING WITH HUMANS by AMACOM in 2004. The follow-up book, A SURVIVAL GUIDE FOR WORKING WITH BAD BOSSES, was published in 2005, followed by DISAGREEMENTS, DISPUTES, AND ALL OUT WAR and A SURVIVAL GUIDE TO MANAGING EMPLOYEES FROM HELL in 2006 and 2007, also from AMACOM.

Scott has been a featured guest on hundreds of TV and radio programs, including *Good Morning America, Oprah, Montel Williams, the O'Reilly Factor, CNN,* and many others. Her books have been featured in numerous articles and book reviews. She has been teaching classes on business, law, organizational behavior, public relations, marketing, management, psychological profiling, and privacy for the University of Notre Dame de Namur and the Investigative Career Program in San Francisco.

She has become a workshop/seminar leader putting on programs based on her latest book WANT IT, SEE IT, GET IT! and on writing, publishing and promoting e-books and print-on-demand books, based on a new company she established to help clients write, publish, market, and sell their own books. As a screenplay writer and indy film producer, she has a feature film, UNBALANCED, in post-production and several others under option. She also writes and produces shorts and trailers.

She received a PhD from the University of California in Sociology; a JD from the University of San Francisco Law School, and MAs in Anthropology, Mass Communications and Organizational/Consumer/Audience Behavior, and Popular Culture and Lifestyles at Cal State, East Bay.

Additional bio and promotional details are at www.ginigrahamscott.com; Information on her production company and scripts and films in development is at www.changemakersproductions.com.

Part 1: Changing Yourself

Chapter 1: Remaking Yourself

This is a good time to think about remaking yourself, since we are in a time of major transformation, and everyone has to change as well to adapt. Some have compared this transformation to the information revolution of two decades ago and to the industrial revolution of the last century. Nothing will ever be the same again.

It is an amazing time in which to live. And today the economy is in turmoil because of all these changes. It's not just a recession, but a time of total transformation. And as technology changes, so does society. And jobs that are being outsourced, simply aren't going to come back. New jobs, new businesses are springing up all the time.

The Need to Change

What all this means is you have to change, too, and think of different ways of changing. In fact, consider several scenarios, so you have different possibilities, like having a Plan A, B, C, D, and even more. This way you have a repertoire of alternatives, so you are prepared no matter what changes occur.

Sure, any change can be a little scary. It takes you out of your comfort zone, what you're used to. But you have to be able to push through those fears to embrace the new. Otherwise, if you're not able to move ahead, you're likely to be left behind, as we move forward into this uncertain new world. It's a little like taking an escalator of change into the future – you don't know exactly where it is going or what floor you are going to get off on. But you have to get onto that escalator, so you can change successfully.

I began thinking about this need to change and remake oneself, when I encountered a major change in my own life. About a week before my recent book came out: WANT IT, SEE IT, GET IT!, my publisher of 8 years and 8 books fired half of the editors and marketing staff.

Why? Because of changes in the publishing industry, because people were reading and buying less books. And more and more people were getting their information from the Internet or e-books. Plus more and more, publishing, like life in general, was being driven by big celebrities and big newsworthy events like the latest scandal. So now there is less interest in books by everyday writers unless they are household names.

Before that event, I had been seeing the growing numbers of people out of work, the rise of pink slip parties, of groups like the Unemployed of Santa Monica. But at first I just felt these developments meant I had a growing pool of people I could hire to work for me at much lower wages than I would normally have to pay.

So for awhile I did staff up with two new employees to pitch my books to publishers and to build my presence on the growing new social media – LinkedIn, Facebook, and Twitter. But gradually I began to realize that this change meant I had to change, too, because publishers weren't snapping up my ideas for new books like before. That's because the industry that I had focused on for three decades was in a terminal slow-down, like newspapers, and things would never be the same. So what if I had published over 50 books? That was yesterday. I had to start thinking of how to change for a new tomorrow.

And it was hard. The decline of publishing and the firings of these editors was like experiencing a death in the family. So I went through a period of mourning and grieving for a few weeks, feeling a little depressed as I came to terms with letting go. I also began to feel a little like I did as a teenager, asking those kind of questions which teenagers do – What am I going to do with my life now?

Well, in a way, this upheaval is what's happening to all of us now. We are experiencing the death of the world as we know it, as a new world struggles to be born. Meanwhile, the world is in the turmoil that we read or hear about in the news everyday – wars in the Middle East, huge waves of immigration, terrorist attacks, job losses, company bankruptcies, and so on. And all the celebrity news, especially Michael Jackson's death, is like a welcome distraction from all these unnerving changing events.

Ways to Change

So think of all this turmoil as a struggle for a new rebirth that will be even more glorious once the transformation is completed. And think about how you can remake yourself for this coming tomorrow.

You simply have to change and push through any fears you have to do so. Otherwise, you might find yourself like a woman I met recently who had lost her job doing special sales for a newspaper. Her job had been to set up special promotional events at schools and universities to promote newspapers sales. She had avoided the first two waves of layoffs, but finally, about 6 months ago, the scythe of job death had hit her. When I asked her what she was doing now, she said she was still looking for another job, but hadn't found anything yet.

So what about using her skills to start her own company? What about doing part-time work for small companies? But her answer was "No...No." No matter what my suggestion was, her answer was the same. She liked working in a large corporate environment. She didn't want to do anything else. She was stuck in denial, stuck in hoping for the return of a past that would never come back. So she's still looking for a job that no longer exists.

In short, the world is rapidly changing and remaking itself. So you have to do so, too. Following is a technique for imagining how you might remake yourself

Remaking Yourself Guided Journey

In this guided visualization, you can think about how to remake yourself – or how to make any other changes in your life. Try taping and listening to it, or read this journey aloud and use the guidelines for going on this journey later. You will be tapping into your intuitive or creative power to help you decide what to do.

To get started, be in a place where you feel comfortable and relaxed. Sit or lie down anywhere, where you can hear the sound of my voice. If possible, do this in a private room where you can shut the door and dim the lights.

Now take some time to relax. Just concentrate on your breathing go in and out, in and out, in and out, so you feel very comfortable, very relaxed, yet can hear the sound of my voice. Yes, you're feeling more and more comfortable, more and more relaxed. Yet, you're aware and alert, so you can hear the sound of my voice.

I'd like you to ask yourself the question: "What do I need to remake about myself? What do I need to change in my work and personal life?" Then, just let the answer come to you. Don't try to think or strive to come up with an answer. Just let the answer come to you and accept whatever comes…

And if you've gotten more than one answer, pick the one response that feels strongest to you. Or ask the question:

"Which of these things should I do first to remake myself?"
Now that you have picked out what you want to change, keep that answer
in mind as you ask yourself the next series of questions.

First, ask yourself: *"Are there any fears, resistances, or blocks standing
in my way of remaking myself?"* Then, see images of any fears, resistances,
or blocks come into your mind. As they do, just notice them. Just let them
appear, like on a screen in front of you...

Then, as you watch this screen, ask yourself: *"Which of these fears is
most important to me now?"* And notice which fear comes up for you. That
is the one you will work on first. While you do so, put any other fears on a
nearby shelf.

Now focus on that fear, and ask yourself: *"What can I do to get rid of or
reduce this fear?"* Don't try to answer, just let the answer come to you...

Then, ask: *"What else can I do to get rid of or reduce this fear?"* Again,
see the answer come to you....

Later, you can put into action whatever insights you have gained from
your intuitive power.

See that fear you have focused on fade away. Just see it get smaller and
smaller, so it finally disappears...

Then, look at the fears you have put on a shelf, and one by one, see each
of those fears get smaller and smaller, until they are all gone...

Later, you will feel these fears are a much smaller part of your life or
even gone. And you can always repeat this process to reduce your fears or
send them away.

And now, feeling that you have overcome any fears standing in your
way, focus on whatever has come to you as what you most need to remake
or change about yourself now in your work or personal life. See whatever it
is very clearly on your screen in your mind's eye...

See yourself changed, since you have already completed that transformation. See yourself as having already changed, and feel how that is for you. Notice where you are, and what else in your life has changed. Notice who you are with if anyone. Just experienced your changed life now, and feel a sense of satisfaction and joy that you have changed as you wanted...

Now, with that image of your transformed self in mind, ask yourself: "What do I need to do now to start remaking myself? What steps to do I need to take to go from where I am now to where I want to be?"...

Notice what answers appear. Don't try to organize these steps into any order. Just let any steps appear to you...

Finally, ask yourself: "What is the first step I need to take?" and see what comes...

Then, ask: "What is the next step?" Again, let the answer come to you.

Lastly, ask: "What is the third step I should take?" See what comes to you...

So now you have the first three steps to take to remake yourself into this new you for today's changing times.

Take a few moments to remind yourself of how you plan to remake yourself and what you will do to get there...

See yourself having achieved this change you want. And you feel good, satisfied, at becoming this new you...

Now, with that feeling of satisfaction, come back to the present. I'm going to count backwards from 5 to 1, and as I do, you'll be coming back into the room. Five, four – coming back now. Three, two, almost back. And one. You are back in the room. So open your eyes, feeling very good and confident that you will be able to make this change in yourself that you want.

Chapter 2: Changing Your Personality and Self-Image

Since more and more people have been using life coaches and participating in programs to transform themselves, this chapter features techniques on how you might change your personality and self-image to improve your relationships and success in the workplace. They incorporate the power of visualization to get what you want – in this case, changing yourself.

The Power of Changing Yourself

To be more successful in a career or business, it helps to have certain personality traits. The ideal traits differ to some extent from occupation to occupation. For instance, a direct sales person needs to be an outgoing, assertive, positive, self-motivated person who takes initiative, and is persuasive and articulate. By contrast, an office worker should be especially conscientious, attentive to detail, organized, and willing to take orders. However, some traits are desirable for everyone—such as being a confident, friendly, creative, high-energy, positive person.

Decide the personality traits or self-image best for you and your own career or business path, and see how your own traits compare. Or determine the areas you want to develop further to get closer to your ideal.

The results can be dramatic if you decide to make some changes—a job more in line with your abilities and interests, improved job performance, a higher income, and more personal power at work and at home. Although we develop certain traits due to experience and because certain traits feel more natural because of our genetic make-up, we can adapt in many ways. One way is to think of how you want to change and practice being that way everyday, until that becomes a habit. After awhile, you may change inside, as that new way of being becomes you.

I have met many people who altered their personalities and self-images for greater success in different ways. For example, a man who managed a small order processing department realized he was too abrasive in dealing with employees. So he worked on becoming more supportive and finding ways to give praise rather than criticism. As a result, he greatly improved both morale and productivity, which led to a nice raise for himself. A school teacher realized she was too impatient and overly critical of people, which made some students resentful and lose interest in their work. So she learned to slow down and become more patient, which resulted in a better behaved class and higher student grades.

Ways to Change Yourself

One way to think about your personality is to see yourself like an actor playing a variety of roles, where you change your personality to adapt to changing circumstances. You may think you have a set personality, but it's like a construct that is continually reaffirmed or recreated as you interact with others.

You have experienced this yourself, when you are one way at work, another at home or when you express different aspects of yourself with different family members and friends. These changes occur because we are all constantly playing different roles in different situations and with different people. We are tough with some people, soft and gentle with others. We act like a little kid with some, like a nurturing parent with others, like an aggressive barracks sergeant with still others. We are all business with some people, wild and crazy with others. And often the situation shapes the role we play—from the business meeting to the office party to the Halloween or New Year's celebrations, when we step into different costumes to take on different roles.

Likewise, when you step into a new and unfamiliar situation, you have to adapt. And this new setting can be a great opportunity to redefine yourself, because people don't already have expectations of who you are. Some examples of this might be when you are asked to take charge in an organization for the first time or you make a career change and the culture of the new field is very different from the one you left. Or you might make changes in yourself to prepare to advance to a new position where you have to take on different tasks and roles.

Another reason for making changes is that you want to change to be more like someone you admire. Or maybe you have a hidden side of yourself you want to express. Or maybe the way you have been acting isn't working. For example, you are too shy and unassertive to get what you want, or you are often difficult to work with because you are too sensitive, irritable, pushy, or aggressive.

Such changes may seem difficult and even scary at first, like stepping into unknown waters. But when you change the way you want to be, the results can lead to all sorts of beneficial results, such as a more satisfying job, greater success in working with others, and increased opportunities.

The key to making these changes is to determine the personality traits that no longer work and figure out the qualities you need to adopt to be successful. Then, you can work on practicing these new traits. Say you have to learn to be more outgoing and comfortable with people. You might put yourself in social situations, such as parties and professional mixers, and force yourself to meet and talk to people. You might volunteer to do things in a social group that force you to relate to people, such as helping to set up programs and introduce speakers, hosting meetings, or doing publicity for the group. Alternatively, to become more introspective and thoughtful, put yourself in such situations. For instance, go on a weekend retreat to a calm and peaceful place or volunteer to do library research for an organization.

The Stages of Changing Yourself

There are four key stages to this process of changing your personality or self-image:

First determine how you want to change; what you want to change or become. Ask yourself: "How would I like to change?" For example, would you like to be more outgoing and dynamic? More warm and affectionate? More articulate? More self-assured in a group? However you want to change, just imagine the qualities you want to eliminate and those you want to develop.

Second, use mental scripting to see yourself in your new role. This procedure lays the groundwork for you to change, because you create a new persona or character for yourself, much like a movie director might do.

Third, practice your mental script to reinforce your new image of yourself. Then, by rehearsing the role over and over again in your mind, you reinforce the reality of this new image. So you see yourself differently when you act in the real world, which helps you act differently as well.

Four, put your new script in action. Now you take the new role and the actions you have imagined yourself doing, and you put them into practice in real-life situations. For instance, if you decide you want to be more outgoing and have imagined yourself acting this way with coworkers, you do just that in the real world. As you do, you keep in mind the image of yourself as a more outgoing friendly person who evokes positive responses from others.

Once you have decided which traits to develop, mental scripting is a great way to develop these qualities. In mental scripting, you see yourself as you want to be and create a scenario in which you play out this role again and again in your mind, until you have developed the assurance that you can do it. For your scenario, use the setting where you want to use your new role.

For example, if you want to develop a more assertive, authoritative personality to become a manager in your company, picture yourself being more assertive and authoritative in your present position and see others responding to you accordingly, such as listening to you more seriously and coming to you frequently for advice. Additionally, see yourself being authoritative and assertive in the new position you want, and notice that people defer to you and respect you. If you want to be a warmer, friendlier person to get along better with co-workers, see yourself doing things in the office to express this warmth and friendliness. For example, visualize yourself offering to make coffee for someone when you make some for yourself or see yourself greeting people with a big smile and a friendly comment. You can use a relaxed, meditative state to imagine whatever scenario you choose.

Another technique is to use an image reinforcer or trigger to remind yourself to act in the way you have imagined in a real-life setting. The way to create this reinforcer is to make an association between the role you want to adopt, the way you want to change to suit that role, and the reminder to make that change. For example, put an object on your desk or picture on your wall that represents the quality you want to develop. To develop the association, look at that object and picture, as you affirm to yourself that you will develop this new quality. Repeat that affirmation again and again to fix that association in your mind. Then, each day, whenever you look at that object or picture, that will remind you to express that quality for yourself.

Finally, besides changing general personality traits, you can target particular behaviors to change in certain situations. You may not change the inner you at first, but you will change the way you respond in a particular role. Then, as you continue to use the same behaviors, that will eventually affect the inner you, so you start to come into alignment with that role.

Even if you feel uncomfortable initially about acting a certain way, eventually you'll own those behaviors and make them part of you. For instance, if you have trouble being authoritative and in charge because you aren't sure people will follow your directions, start by visualizing yourself being a more powerful and authoritative person. Then, start acting that way in everyday life, and after awhile, you will feel comfortable in your new role.

Create your own visualization to help you clearly imagine how you want to change and the steps you might take to achieve those changes in yourself and your life.

Part 2: Improving Your Relationship to Money and the Economy

Chapter 3: Improving Your Relationship with Money and Work

Since the turmoil in the economy has been very much in the news, this chapter features techniques on how to improve your relationship with money and work, whether you do additional work on the side, start your own business, or engage in bartering. Because of all the changes in the economy and society, this is a good time to think about using your skills to find new work opportunities, use barter to swap your skills for the skills you need from someone else, or launch a home based business that can take off as the economy soars again. Or maybe you can do a combination of all three approaches. In a subsequent chapter, I'll describe ways to simplify your life, including how to spend less and save more.

**Finding a Fit Between Your Skills
and Today's Market**

First, whatever your work situation, think about how your skills might help people with what they need or want today. This way, you find a fit between what you can offer and people's needs and wants. For example, hundreds of new entrepreneurs have been launching Internet start-ups with limited up-front costs and high potential, such as writing an e-book on a topic people want to know about, like making money using the social media.

What might you do to appeal to today's market? Think of start-up possibilities you could launch yourself -- or look into direct sales programs you could represent which have products or services people might need and want.

Questions to Ask if You Are Looking for More Work

If you are looking for work assignments, some questions to ask are these: assignments, some key questions to ask are these:

• What kind of skills and talents do I have? Later you can rank your preferences.

• What types of industries might be able to use my job skills?

• What steps can I take now to approach people in these industries about getting work from clients?

• How can I best present myself to offer these skills?

• What new skills might I develop which are needed now? How can I develop these skills as quickly as possible?

• What might I do to show that I can apply these new skills in this new field?

Once you determine what you want to do, show how you can apply these skills, such as by creating a portfolio to show what you can do. Also, get testimonials from individuals or organizations where you have used these skills, whether paid or as a volunteer.

Creating a Start-Up Business

As a first step, think of start-up possibilities you could launch yourself -- or look into direct sales programs you could represent with products or services people might need and want.

But a caution: if you go into a direct sales, network marketing, or multi-level marketing company, be cautious of scammers promising riches through pyramid schemes. Look for companies with solid products or services that people really need or want to buy, aside from any money making opportunities. These should be things that you or others would buy even if there was no opportunity to make money. These should be products or services that provide real value.

Another caution is that normally, only 5-10% of the consumers for a product or service will seriously market it to make money. If most people are joining for the business opportunity, that's a warning sign the business could turn into a pyramid scheme where there is little interest in the product or service itself. So soon the pyramid will collapse as people turn to something else to make money.

If you are drawn to being an entrepreneur, this is an especially good time to start a new business, since you can hire talented people at lower than usual starting wages, because so many people are out of work. That's what I found when I launched a number of new projects in L.A. during the depths of the recession. In fact, there was a growing network of pink slip parties and support groups for the newly unemployed, which provided a fertile field for hiring skilled talent. Or if you are willing to take a pay cut yourself, use this downturn to learn new skills in a new field by working for someone who is starting a new company. Then, if you can help the company become successful and expand, there will be opportunities for promotion and increased wages as the recession ends and the company grows.

So what do you want to do now? Here are some questions to ask to help you decide:

- What kind of skills and talents do I have? List your strongest ones and prioritize them by ranking them from 1 (highest) to 5 (lowest) based on which skills you would most like to use now.

- What do people especially need now that they aren't getting from other companies or individuals?

- How can I apply my skills and talents to provide products or services that will help others fulfill their needs and wants? Ask this question for each of your top skills and talents first; then go on to the next highly ranked group for still more ideas.

- What steps can I take to develop, promote, and provide these products and services? Create a list of steps to take.

- What do I need to put these steps into action, such as what employees, materials, or contacts do I need to take these actions?

Finally, put these steps into action. Start now by taking the first step.

Creating a Home-Based Business

If you decide to create a home-based business, here are some steps to optimize your chances for success.

First, set up a dedicated space in your home for your business. Find a place where you can close the door, so you feel like you are going to work – and anyone else in your house will know this.

Second, equip your work area with the necessary materials for your type of business. Visualize what you are going to be doing each day, and create a list for what you need. Pare it down to the basic essentials if you have a limited budget. When you go shopping, look for store specials, no-interest loans for purchases, or discounts to keep down your costs.

Third, to make your home-based business more efficient, create some boundaries with your family and friends, so they know you are working at certain times and don't distract you with non-work calls or questions. Explain that your work time and work space is for work only, as if you were going to work in an office.

Fourth, work out a schedule for when you will check your e-mails, such as every two or three hours, so you can concentrate on your work between making e-mail checks. Let people know that if something is crucial and needs fast action to call you; otherwise they should contact you by e-mail. This way, you cut down on the distractions from too frequent e-mail checks and phone calls, so you have a solid block of time to work.

Fifth, dedicate about 2-3 hours a day for marketing your product or service, including going to networking events.

Sixth, set up a Website for your business which looks professional. To keep your costs down, use a hosting service offering templates, where you can choose from several hundred Website formats; then customize it for your business. This way you don't have to start from scratch to build your Website. Feature the products or services you want to sell on your Website and make it easy to buy them, such as by setting up Amazon or Paypal payment account, so people can easily click and pay. If possible, set up a merchant account with your bank, so people can pay by credit cards, too.

Seventh, find ways to promote your business inexpensively to keep down costs. For example, create flyers, brochures, or catalog sheets about your products or services, and print them on an as need basis from your computer. Then, if people seem responsive and your business takes off, invest in getting a larger print-run of several hundred or more materials.

Eighth, take some of flyers with you wherever you go. Then, give them out as appropriate to people you meet at networking events, business expos, or in your day to day activities.

Ninth, look for opportunities to turn the conversation to what you are marketing; then if people are interested, give out your flyers, brochures, catalog sheets, or a business card. Include your Website and email on all your materials. You can order these materials inexpensively through a number of Internet companies, such as Vista Prints.

Using Bartering to Increase Your Income

Consider bartering your products and services for products and services you need, if you can make a direct exchange. Or consider joining a bartering service. This way, rather than spending money, you can trade your skills, services, or products for something you want from someone else.

This bartering system predates the use of money, and during a recession in the early 1980s, numerous bartering clubs sprang up, so people out of work or having financial problems could increase the funds available to them. Then, as the economy recovered, interest in these bartering clubs declined and many closed, as people rejoined the mainstream economy.

Today, this bartering idea is growing again, so you might find one in your area, or consider starting a barter service as a new business. It can be a home-based business, too.

In short, there are all sorts of ways to increase your money or spending power, while taking precautions so you don't get led into a money-making scheme that costs you money.

In the next section, I'll show you a technique for coming up with new ways to increase your money and spending power.

Volunteering to Acquire New Skills and Opportunities

You might also consider volunteering to open up doors to new types of work. To do so, think about how you can volunteer to do something where the work is needed and where your skills and interests make this task a good fit. Volunteering is a good way to learn new skills, as well as keep you busy and fulfilled, because you are making a contribution. Later you can use that experience to help you get a paying job – or get clients to pay you for using these skills on their behalf.

So where should you volunteer? For ideas, look through the listings of local organizations in your areas seeking volunteers. Or create your own volunteer activity, where you find a need and fill it. Note the skills you use as a volunteer and keep track of the people you meet along the way.

Then, look for people who have projects or part-time work using that skill. Or you may be able to turn your volunteer work into a paid job, once the organization is ready to hire again. Later, when the economy revives and there are new job openings, you have a whole new repertoire of skills to offer. And prospective employers will like your altruistic, can-do spirit, increasing your chances of getting a paying job.

The Power of Visualization to Improve Your Relationship to Money and Work

Using visualization can be a powerful tool to help you improve your relationship to money and find new work.

Say your field has been undergoing lay-offs or restructuring, so you can't find the kind of work as in the past. Think about how the skills and talents you have can be applied in a new setting. Or think about what new skills you need to learn to work at something you'd like to do. Or turn your skills into a service you can provide.

Visualization can help by enabling you to imagine the possibilities, so you can come up with more ideas to choose from and then feel more strongly and knowingly what to do. The advantage of using visualization techniques as you ask these questions is that you tap into your intuition or the creative force within you. So you don't just think of but see and experience the answers. This way you can come up with more and better ideas, and you can better see what to do to turn these ideas into action.

To prepare for the visualization process, get some paper and a pen to write with, so you can note your great ideas. Or use a recording device, if you'd prefer to say your ideas aloud rather than write them. Then, find a comfortable quiet place where you can be alone for about 20-30 minutes.

Now get relaxed and imagine there is a screen in front of you where you will see the answers in the form of images or words in your mind's eye. Then, ask yourself a series of questions, such as the ones already listed, and don't try to judge or rate the answers in any way. You'll do that later, when it comes time to prioritize and choose.

Improving Your Relationship with Money and Work Guided Journey

The following guided visualization will help you imagine how to improve your relationship with money. Try taping it and listen to it, or read this journey aloud and use the guidelines for going on this journey later. You will be tapping into your intuitive or creative power to help you decide what to do.

To get started, be in a place where you feel comfortable and relaxed. Sit or lie down anywhere, where you can hear the sound of my voice.

If possible, do this in a private room where you can shut the door and dim the lights.

Now take some time to relax. Just concentrate on your breathing going in and out, in and out, in and out, so you feel very comfortable, very relaxed. Yet, you're aware and alert, so you can hear my voice.

Now, ask yourself the question: "What can I do to bring more money into my life." Then, let any answers come to you. Don't try to think or strive to come up with an answer. Just let the answers come to you and accept whatever comes. Just keep imagining all the different ways in which you can bring more money into your life...

To help you come up with even more ideas, I'll suggest some different possibilities you can think about.

First, think about how your skills might be turned into ways to create new work or business opportunities for yourself. Even if you haven't used these skills in a long time, think about what you can do now. Ask yourself: "What kind of skills and talents do I have that are especially useful now?"

Now think about what you consider your strongest skills. What skills would you most like to use now in your work or business?...

Think about what people need today that they aren't getting from other companies or individuals. As the ideas flash into your mind, think about how you might use your skills and talents to fill these needs and wants. Do this for your strongest skills first — then go on to some of your other skills....

Next imagine what steps you can take to develop, promote, and provide these products and services? Ask yourself: "What do I need to put these steps into action, such as employees, materials, or contacts with others?" Then, see yourself putting these steps into action. Later you can actually do what you visualize now...

Now, think about what you might do if you were going to start a business. Imagine what it might look like. What kinds of products or services might you offer?....

Or if you are going to do marketing and promotion for a direct sales business, what kind of business would that be? What kinds of products or services would you be marketing and promoting?...

Take some time to see yourself running your own business or participating in a direct sales company. Imagine what your typical day might be like. See yourself going through your daily activities...

See yourself promoting your own business or the products or services you represent. What do you do? Where do you go? Maybe you need to create some flyers, brochures, or catalog sheets and take them with you. See yourself praising your skills, products, or services to others. As you do, you notice that others are impressed with what you are saying. They are very receptive and enthusiastic. And you feel even more charged up, energetic, and enthused yourself...

Notice what you might do to get more work or business, so you can overcome some resistance you encounter due to the recession. For example, maybe you can hire someone at a low rate to help you look for work by contacting potential employers or clients. Maybe you can go to some events for the newly unemployed to hire some help or look for ideas and inspiration. Maybe you can reduce your usual rates for a short time to get some work or volunteer to get new skills in a new field. Maybe you can engage in bartering for other products and services which you need. Just take some time to think about what you might do...

Next, imagine you are setting up some space in your home or office for whatever you have decided to do. See yourself organizing the area and setting up files... See yourself going shopping to get whatever else you need....

Now see yourself setting up a schedule for what you will do to build or promote yourself or your business...

Next imagine what you are going to do in the next day or the next two days to get more work, start a new business, or expand your current business. Make this commitment to yourself to start now...

Finally, see yourself as having accomplished your goals. You have gotten more work or have started or grown your business. So you feel very good, very successful, very confident for the future.

Now with this feeling of accomplishment and satisfaction, come back to the present. I'm going to count backwards from 5 to 1, and as I do, you'll come back into the room. Five, four – coming back now. Three, two, almost back. And one. You are back in the room. So open your eyes, feeling very good..

Later, take some time to write down some of these ideas for getting more work or expanding your business and think about how to put them into action.

Chapter 4: Simplifying Your Life

Now is an ideal time to think about ways to simplify your life to improve it, because of the economic transformation we are experiencing. The recession has been going on for over a year, and it seems likely to continue, despite signs it has been easing.

In a way, this economic upheaval is a correction to the excesses of the last decade or so. Both our national and personal debt has increased, because credit was so easy. You could easily get credit cards – I got repeated offers to sign on for more and more cards. And if you wanted to buy a house you couldn't afford, it was usually easy to get a stated income loan. You could say whatever your income was, and get all kinds of loans to help you afford the house, such as a no interest loan for five years.

Meanwhile, books about how you could imagine whatever you wish for and get it helped feed the fantasy. Certainly, using your imagination **does** help you get what you want – in fact I wrote a book: WANT IT, SEE IT, GET IT! that helps you do just that. However, beyond imagining the end goal, you have to imagine the steps to take to get there, and you have to do a reality check to make sure what you are wishing for is realistic.

So **do** continue to set goals and work on getting what you want. But at the same time, recognize today's new reality, which suggests a need to slow down, assess what's most important, and cut back to emphasize your true priorities.

From time to time, in the last few decades, people have talked about the value of living more simply. But generally, these advocates have been only a small minority of people who have taken steps to simplify their lives, such as joining together in some form of community living – like a rural commune or share houses in a city. In other cases, people have given up their cars to reduce pollution or cut back on expenses. Other strategies have involved creating buying clubs to buy and share large quantities of food and supplies at a discount.

Now, the need to reduce expenses and live more simply has become more critical for everyone. Just think of the hundreds of thousands of people experiencing foreclosures. Many of these people might have avoided this situation had they thought of ways to cut down their expenses and get rid of unnecessary or rarely used things in advance.

Steps to Simplifying Your Life

It may be that you may continue to have difficulty in finding a job, getting as much part-time work as before, or charging as much as you used to. But if you can reduce your expenses, you'll be better able to manage each month.

How? Here are some suggestions.

First, reduce the space you need to live in by getting rid of extra books, clothes, and other items which you rarely use. In some cases, you can sell them, such as selling your books to used bookstores or book collectors, many of whom now sell on line. If you have clothes in good condition, you might put them on consignment in a resale shop. You might also post items for sale on e-bay or go to an e-bay consignment shop which will do everything for you in return for a commission – about 35%.

Secondly, your cleared out space may mean that you can live in a smaller and less expensive space – or you may have space for a roommate or housemate that can cut your rent payment down or contribute to your mortgage payment.

Thirdly, you can cut back on some of your expenses that aren't necessary and replace them with less expensive alternatives. For instance, if you've gotten accustomed to $3 and $4 lattes, maybe a $1 to $2 cup of coffee would taste just as good. Maybe instead of two drinks at a bar or nightclub, take one. Try going out a little earlier so you make the club's happy hour and enjoy happy hour prices – often a few dollars less. Or if a restaurant serves big portions, share a large entry or a salad with an extra plate, instead of getting much more than you can eat.

Another area for cut-backs is in luxury spending for new styles, where what you currently own is perfectly good. For instance, maybe you don't need that coat, pair of shoes, slacks, or whatever you might buy because it looks good. Or maybe you can dress up what you are wearing with different accessories, like a scarf or jewelry, rather than buying something new.

Still another way to cut down is to go to a next-to-new shop, Goodwill, other kind of thrift shops, or outlet malls. Often you can find barely or never worn items there that look really good for a few dollars instead of a spending ten times as much for something new. And this is a good way to recycle perfectly good items that reduce the drain of resources for the whole planet. You can build a large wardrobe this way, providing you with plenty of variety, and no one needs to know if you don't want to tell them. Alternatively, in some circles, you can show off your good taste in buying inexpensively – and people will complement you for your economic savvy.

Another way to reduce expenses is to entertain by having a potluck dinner, where everyone brings something to share. You can make these especially fun and creative if you have a theme – like East Asian night, where everyone cooks up something from a country in East Asia. You might add some simple decorations or music that ties in with the theme, too – or invite people to contribute.

You can save money when you go out, too, such as by finding less expensive restaurants. Or if you go to a nightclub, go early or on certain nights to avoid a cover charge.

Still other possibilities are finding different types of recreational activities that cost less or are free. One possibility is going to a nearby park or nature preserve. You might organize a fun barbecue at the beach, where participants bring their own food to share, and those who are musical might bring guitars, drums, and other instruments. You might hike around your neighborhood (assuming it is safe) instead of walking on a treadmill at the gym. Look for free or inexpensive fairs and festivals in your area, too.

You might also join or organize a group of people who share a similar interest in cutting back, such as through a connections organization like Meetup.com. For instance, join or start a group on Under $10 or $15 Ethnic Dining. Go with groups to events, so you can get a reduced price for going to the event.

Reducing your travel costs can provide even more savings. For example, look for ways to share rides to work or to recreational activities. Offer to drive others to events you are attending in return for them contributing to the gas and tolls. And where you can, work at home using your computer, e-mail, and phone, instead of driving to the office. In fact, there is software and Websites that enable you to set up meetings with others, such as Skype. All you need is a Webcam and a mike, and even without a Webcam, you can participate on the phone.

Should you have a second place which you don't go to very much, maybe you could rent it out when you aren't there or sell it.

In short, you can easily cut down your less important expenses, so you have more to spend on what is most important to you. Cutting back also means you will need to work less to make your monthly minimum;

you'll have less need to draw on your equity line or credit cards, so you can cut down on your interest payments. And you may be able to travel more and engage in more fun leisure time activities, because you need to work less each month.

Following is a technique for imagining how you might simplify your life.

Simplifying Your Life Guided Journey

Now I'd like to lead you in a guided visualization in which you can think about how to simplify your life and cut back on expenses. Try taping it and listen to it, or read this journey aloud and use the guidelines for going on this journey later. You will be tapping into your intuitive or creative power to help you decide what changes to make to make your life simpler.

To get started, be in a place where you feel comfortable and relaxed. Sit or lie down anywhere, where you can imagine the sound of my voice. If possible, do this in a private room where you can shut the door and dim the lights.

Take some time to relax. Just concentrate on your breathing going in and out, in and out, in and out, so you feel very comfortable, very relaxed. Yet, you're aware and alert, so you can hear the sound of my voice.

Now, I'd like you to ask yourself the question: "What can I do to simplify my life or cut back on expenses? What do I need less of in my life?" Then, let any answers come to you. Don't try to think or strive to come up with an answer. Just let the answers come to you and accept whatever comes.

You may get a number of answers. And that's fine. Just keep imagining all the different ways in which you can make your life simpler and spend less...

Now, from all the ideas you have gotten, pick the one way that feels strongest to you. Or ask the question: "Which of these things should I do first to simply my life or spend less?"

Then, with that idea in mind, ask yourself: "What steps do I need to take to put that idea into action?" For example, you may need to set up a schedule. You may need to make some phone calls to let others know you are making changes. You may need to talk to a partner about the changes you hope to make so you can get an agreement. You may need to put away your credit cards or make an appointment to meet with your banker. Whatever it is, take some time to think about what you have to do to make that change...

Think about the second thing you would like to do to simplify your life and spend less. Again, with that idea in mind, ask yourself the same question: "What steps do I need to take to put that idea into action?" Again, take some time to think about all the steps you need to take to make that change.

Next, think about the second thing you would like to do to simplify your life and spend less, and ask yourself the same question: "What steps do I need to take to put that idea into action." And again, take some time to think about all the steps you need to take to make that change.

Later, you can write down these ideas and the steps to put them into action. Should you still have other ideas, you can similarly pick each one and work out the steps to take.

So now, imagine that you have taken all the steps you have imagined, and see yourself living in this changed way. See yourself living more simply and spending less each day, week, or month.

Notice how you feel much better having made these changes. You feel more relaxed and experience less stress. You feel more confident and sure of yourself. You feel freer and more independent when you think about money. You feel less pressure on you to do what you don't want to do, and *you feel you have more choices and more freedom in choosing what you **do** want to do.*

So take some time now to experience all these changes and feel more satisfied, fulfilled, happier in your life...

Also, notice the positive ways in which these changes have affected the people you are with...

So again, take some time to see yourself engaging in these new activities with others, and see yourself enjoying these changes in your life with them...

You have made the changes you want to simplify your life and cut down on your expenses. And you feel good, satisfied, at becoming this new you...

So now, with this feeling of satisfaction, come back to the present. I'm going to count backwards from 5 to 1, and as I do, you'll be coming back into the room. Five, four — coming back now. Three, two, almost back. And one. You are back in the room. So open your eyes, feeling very good and confident that you will be able to make this change in yourself that you want.

Part 3: Adding More Fun to Your Life

Chapter 5: Adding More Celebration to Your Life

Finding new ways to celebrate and add more celebration to your life seems especially important now, given the grim state of the economy and the world. We need more ways to step outside the mundane everyday reality to have more fun and feel better about ourselves and our daily experiences.

The Power and Pervasiveness of Celebration

The value of celebration has long been recognized in every culture, going back to the beginnings of human history and even before. It is closely linked with the use of ritual and play, which even many animals do. A ritual is a regularly performed action, and often it is done as part of a religious service or personal spiritual practice. Celebration is often incorporated in such religious rituals, such as when a prayer session or meditation concludes with a sense of joy and liberation. Likewise, play, which involves engaging in a free spirited fun activity, can incorporate a celebration or conclude with one. An example is when a game ends in a victory which calls for a celebration.

Celebrations can also give special recognition and fun to almost anything – from birthdays and holidays to the successful completion of any kind of tasks in business or at work.

You might think of celebrations as those special occasions that add a sense of excitement, awe, joy, or other types of heightened emotional release. They are a way to brighten and add meaning to your life, and they bring people together in a spirit of community and bonding. Without celebration life would be truly drab and monotonous – just doing a series of routine tasks day after day. It would be a little like being on a factory line that keeps going, going, and going and never ends. You would feel bored and unstimulated, living but not really alive. But a celebration, even a short one lasting just a few minutes, helps to recharge the mind and the soul.

Hence, the power of all sorts of celebration throughout history. There are celebrations to mark the passage from one stage of life to another – such as baptisms to welcome a new child to the family and community, birthdays, coming of age ceremonies like barmitzvahs and fraternity hazings, marriage ceremonies, seasonal holidays like Easter and Christmas, and Saints Days in the Catholic Faith. There are days when one can be someone else, such as during Mardi Gras and Halloween. There are celebrations to welcome newcomers to a group, organization, company, or neighborhood. There are parties to support or celebrate the success of a team, like tailgate parties and victory parties. Other parties are for achievements and promotions, still others for retiring or leaving a group.

In short, almost any event you can think of has a celebration associated with it – and there are special celebrations around the world associated with a particular industry, such as fleet days when the boats launch; launch parties for when a new company begins; and more.

Ways to Create More Celebration in Your Life

Individuals, families, and blocks of neighbors may create their own celebrations, too, for different occasions. For instance, you might create a personal celebration to reward yourself for achieving some goal; your family might arrange to celebrate a special family day, such as by having a family picnic, graduation party, or outing at the beach. Your neighbors might organize a block party or become part of a network of block parties, such as National Night Out, which is sponsored by law enforcement to encourage neighbors to bond together and protect one another against crime.

I even wrote a book which features many different types of celebrations at work called: ENJOY: 101 LITTLE WAYS TO ADD FUN TO YOUR WORK EVERYDAY. For example, you can give yourself a quick reward at the end of completing a task or a certain amount of work. You can take a stretch or exercise break and imagine that you are celebrating some kind of achievement while you do. If you are doing routine work that doesn't involve much concentration, you might imagine yourself engaging in some fun activity.

Or you might find ways to make work more fun for everyone, such as by having a party where people decorate their workplaces. Other possibilities include organizing a special dress-up day, creating a bingo awards game for people's work, taking a goofy break to unwind, having a time at a meeting for people to brag about themselves, and beginning or ending a meeting with an inspirational story.

Still other possibilities are having a creative gift exchange, organizing a humorous theme contest or event, setting up an office skit or poetry slam party, and having a fashion show. Or try devising a workplace scavenger hunt, having a diversity day celebration, and organizing a creativity day where team members come up with creative uses for a series of objects.

Some other ideas for fun celebrations include creating a match-up game to help people learn about each other, having a rewards and recognition contest, using humorous gifts for office celebrations, and finding novel ways to recognize employees. Some more suggestions are putting on a surprise party for a special occasion, organizing a come-as a character day, creating a be-a-kid for a day event, and organizing a theme party featuring a fun place, such as a Down Under Australia party or Polynesian luau.

If you travel, you will find opportunities to participate in a wide variety of celebrations in different communities throughout the U.S. and the world. Just pick up the local daily or weekly newspaper and see what's going on. For example, when I was in Southern California, one of the special celebrations I attended was a party to look for and welcome the grunions, a small fish that arrives in mass on the beach at certain times of the year to spawn. Another event was a Harvest Festival put on by a local college which featured a walk through a mysterious corn maze where costumed figures jumped out from the corn to startle everyone. And one of my favorites was a monthly drumming ceremony on the playa, where people came with their drums and rattles and danced and chanted around a bonfire.

In short, there are all sorts of ways to add celebration to your life – from what you do individually to what you do with friends, family, neighbors, your whole community, and the nation.

And you can not only engage in celebrations with others, but you can use your imagination to create personal celebrations in your mind. In turn, such celebrations not only add fun and excitement to your life, but they can help you become close to and bond with others and add meaning to your life. Also, when you use your imagination to come up with and experience celebrations, you are exercising and expanding your creativity, as well as stimulating your mental abilities, particularly your ability to visualize and plan.

Following is a technique for adding more celebration to your life.

Adding More Celebration to Your Life Guided Journey

Now I'd like to lead you in a guided visualization in which you can think about how to add more celebration to your life. Try taping it and listen to it, or read this journey aloud and use the guidelines for going on this journey later. You will be tapping into your intuitive or creative power to help you imagine different types of celebrations you can add to your life to create more excitement, fun, meaning, and bonding with others.

To get started, be in a place where you feel comfortable and relaxed. Sit or lie down anywhere, where you can imagine the sound of my voice. If possible, do this in a private room where you can shut the door and dim the lights.

Take some time to relax. Just concentrate on your breathing going in and out, in and out, in and out, so you feel very comfortable, very relaxed. Yet, you're aware and alert, so you can hear the sound of my voice.

Now ask yourself the question: "What can I do to add more celebration into my life?" Then, let any answers come to you. Don't try to think or strive to come up with an answer. Just let the answers come to you and accept whatever comes. Just keep imagining all the different ways in which you can add more celebration into your life...

To help you come up with even more ideas, think about the ways you can add celebration in different situations...

First, ask yourself: "What can I do to create more personal celebrations for myself at home?" Just let the answers come to you...

Next, imagine what kind of celebrations you might create with your friends or family. Let your mind go, so you feel free to experience whatever you want...

Then, see yourself at work, and imagine how you can liven up your day with individual celebrations...

Now imagine what you might do to create celebrations with other employees whether you are a co-worker or a boss.

Imagine that you are putting on a party with a theme. Think of the first theme idea that comes to mind Imagine different ways you might express that theme. For instance, imagine people wearing different kinds of costumes....Imagine a magnificent spread of food that ties in with that theme.... Imagine people playing music, putting on skits, or playing games that reflect that theme.

Now imagine yourself participating in a street or community festival. It's a gala occasion. Lots of people from your house or neighborhood are there enjoying themselves. Kids are running around playing. Maybe a band is playing music. See yourself walking around, meeting others, enjoying yourself at this big celebration....

See yourself traveling. You are in another city, state, or country, and there is a big celebration going on. Imagine that you are going to this event by yourself or with others. You hear music; you see booths with different types of food; there are people displaying art and jewelry. So now walk around and experience this celebration...

Now imagine that you are the center of a big celebration celebrating you... Think of all the things you have to celebrate about yourself... These might be your accomplishments... the great people in your life...your home.... the neighborhood or community where you live. Just celebrate anything you want to celebrate about yourself. Think of this like a celebration of thanksgiving, gratitude, or appreciation – where you are celebrating all the great things you can think of about yourself. So take some time to experience and enjoy this celebration of you...

So now, with this feeling of enjoyment and satisfaction, come back to the present. I'm going to count backwards from 5 to 1, and as I do, you'll be coming back into the room. Five, four – coming back now. Three, two, almost back. And one. You are back in the room. So open your eyes, feeling very good.

Later, take some time to write down some of these ideas for celebrations and think about how you can add your favorite ideas to your own life.

Part 4: Having a Better Environment Around You

Chapter 6: Improving Your Relationship with Nature

Since we have rapidly been losing touch with nature, as cities expand and wilderness areas are rapidly being destroyed, this chapter focuses on how you might improve your relationship with nature and the wilderness.

The Need for a Closer Relationship with Nature Today

I know for many people like me, the wilderness seems very far away. It's something we see in films that involve struggles against the wilderness, like *Into the Wild*, a film about a young man who goes to Alaska to find himself, but is totally unprepared for wilderness living and dies of starvation. Another of these films is *Grizzly Adams*, about a young man and his girl friend, who spend a summer communing with and filming the bears, only to be eaten by them. Sometimes we see some nature films on the Discovery Channel, in the theaters, or on DVD like *Earth*. Or we see the wild as a backdrop for human conflict and conniving, such as on *Survivor* or *I'm a Celebrity, Get Me Out of Here*. Then, too, we may see a bit of the urbanized wild in a city zoo, where a small piece of land is designed to resemble the African savannah or a tropical rainforest.

But in all of these cases, we don't fully have a wilderness experience – mainly we just observe others having the experience – and in some cases, even the animals in that small bit of wilderness don't have a true wilderness experience either.

Unfortunately, the wilderness is being rapidly reduced today, due to the spread of the urban and suburban metropolis, expanded logging and farming, and growing settlements due to increasing populations. So more and more, the wilderness is being cut down and bulldozed away, and many thousands of species that live in the wild have been lost in the process – about 10,000 each year, as I recently read.

At the same time, the growing stresses of urban and suburban life mean it's more important than ever to experience the natural wilderness oneself. That's because the wilderness has a calming, restorative influence. It's a way to get away from city noises and traffic and from living in close proximity to hundreds or thousands of neighbors, store owners, and others in everyday life.

Getting in touch with the wilderness is also a way to get in touch with your roots, since our heritage, our DNA, derives from that past. Until about 10,000 years ago, all around the world, our ancestors were still living as hunters and gathers. So we still draw on that past for our reflexes, our ability to sense and perceive, our impulse to respond to fear by fight or flight, and our basic need to love, nurture, and bond with others.

How to Get More In Touch with Nature Today

Thus, this is a good time to think about how you might get more in touch with nature, and where possible, the wilderness itself. While it may not be possible to strike out for the wild yourself, at least you can take some steps to bring more of nature into your life. Here are some suggestions.

First, if you can get away for a week or two, consider going with a small wilderness tour group into a wilderness area, such as Alaska, Yosemite, or the Grand Tetons. Or if you are adventurous, go with a friend or two. But it's best not to go on your own for safety reasons. The advantage of a small group, such as arranged through a wilderness travel company or a college or university travel program, is that you are led by an experienced leader with wilderness skills. That group can also provide you with much of the equipment you'll need, from tents to cooking gear, besides whatever you get on your own.

Second, you may find some weekend or day trips to nearby woods or mountains offered through a college or high school extension program or travel agency.

Another possibility is to get involved with a local hiking or adventure travel club. You can find these groups listed in your community newspaper or in the weekly freebies published in some towns. Another place to find these groups is Meetup.com – just put in your zip code and look for groups within 10 to 25 miles from you. Some areas will have a "linkup" group (which is not the same as "linkedin") such as the Bay Area Link Up and LA Link Up, where local hosts post events they are leading.

Another suggestion is to join a local birding or hiking group, which you might find through these community resources. Then, when you go out on a trip with the group, see how many different kinds of birds you can find. Afterwards, you'll find you pay more attention to the birds around you, too, as I discovered after I joined a birding group organized through a local adult education center. Before, I didn't pay much attention to any birds flying; they were basically background. But now I became very aware of them, particularly since I could now name different ones. They weren't just birds anymore, but hummingbirds, swallows, crows, ravens, hawks, cranes, gulls, and other species, which I noticed that crossed my path.

Such hiking and birding groups will make you aware of other types of flora and fauna, too, as you walk around. And you can find other groups that specialize in looking for certain types of animals.

You might also consider walking around your neighborhood, if it's an area with plenty of trees, bushes, and flowers. Or walk or drive to a nearby park and walk around that.

If you are near a riding stable with a nature trail, try renting a horse for a few hours and ride along these trails by yourself or in a small group. Or initially go out with an instructor, so you feel comfortable and safe before going out on your own.

Still another possibility, if you have an artistic bent, is to join a local art group that goes out on photography or painting expeditions to nearby parks, meadows, and wooded areas for a day, weekend, or week. Or go out with your camera or painting equipment on your own. I found just having a camera with me helped me look more closely at the natural world around me.

Or even if you don't have a camera or paintbrush and canvas, try imagining frames around the natural images you see. It's a way of focusing your attention, so you observe more closely and see more.

Another approach is to take up gardening, whether you do it in your own backyard or join a local gardening club. Then, as you garden, pay attention to the natural world around you. Notice the birds and squirrels that come to visit your garden. Pay attention to any passing beetles, spiders, bees, and other insects.

Or how about participating in some sports that take you out into nature? For example, instead of skiing down slopes with the crowds, try cross country skiing. Or try rafting, canoeing, or kayaking through rivers, lakes, or streams. Other possibilities include hang-gliding, rock climbing, and mountain climbing.

If you enjoy games, you can combine competition with getting out in nature, such as by playing paintball or laser tag in the woods. You'll find some local organizations that do this, such as lasertag.org, if you do a search on google or through connections group like Meetup. Generally, you can be a complete novice to join the fun. For example, I signed up to participate in a laser tag event for the first time over the Labor Day weekend. It was held in a large nature preserve near the San Francisco Airport. Far in the distance, cars whizzed by on the freeway and planes took off and landed. But the Juniper Serra Park where we battled it out was like a different world of trails, meadows, and woods.

Participants were able to join as their own 6-person team, and the organizers filled up the groups that were short one or two players with those who came on their own on. The event began with a brief orientation session describing the rules of the game and how to operate the guns. Then, we were off and running in a game of capture the flag – and to do so, we tried to kill our opponents with laser shots at a sensor we each wore on our heads and guns. It took five shots to wound and kill an opponent. But fortunately, once you were dead, you could quickly get up, get your gun reloaded, and play again. Though there was a small prize for the team with the highest score, the fun was in the playing itself and having a chance to run around in nature, while shooting or getting shot.

Finally, even if you can't actually go out into nature, you can always use your imagination to take you wherever you want to go. It's a way to experience nature in your mind more fully, than by sitting back like a spectator and seeing a nature film in the theater or on TV. Or if you do watch a film or look at nature pictures in a book, you can do so even more proactively, by projecting yourself into the scene, so you experience what you are looking at like you are there.

In short, there are all sorts of ways to increase your connection with nature and the wilderness.

Following is a technique for coming up with new ways to improve your own relationship with nature.

Improving Your Relationship with
Nature Guided Journey

Now I'd like to lead you in a guided visualization in which you can think about how to improve your relationship with nature. Try taping it and listen to it, or read this journey aloud and use the guidelines for going on this journey later. You will be tapping into your intuitive or creative power to help you imagine different ways of relating more closely to nature.

To get started, be in a place where you feel comfortable and relaxed. Sit or lie down anywhere, where you can imagine the sound of my voice. If possible, do this in a private room where you can shut the door and dim the lights.

Take some time to relax. Just concentrate on your breathing going in and out, in and out, in and out, so you feel very comfortable, very relaxed. Yet, you're aware and alert, so you can hear the sound of my voice.

Now, ask yourself the question: "What can I do to improve my relationship with nature." Then, let any answers come to you. Don't try to think or strive to come up with an answer. Let the answers come to you and accept whatever comes. Just keep imagining all the different ways in which you can improve your relationship with nature...

To help you come up with even more ideas, I'll suggest some different possibilities you can think about.

First, I'd like you to think about what you can do to get out into nature or the wilderness more? When might you get some time to do this? Where might you go? Imagine yourself planning or taking this trip now.

Now, imagine yourself actually there. See yourself in the mountains, hiking on a meadow or walking through the woods. Notice the trees and plants around you...Smell the freshness in the air...Go touch a tree or the leaves of some plants...Feel the texture...Experience the strength of the tree or the fluidity of the leaf as you touch it....Now imagine that the tree or plant might speak to you or has a message for you about something...It's like you are getting insights or wisdom from nature...Listen closely to this... What does that tree or plant say?...And how might you use that message in your daily life?

Now imagine you are a trip to see the birds or other animals in your area. Imagine that you are carrying binoculars or a camera and perhaps a notebook to write down what you see. You may be on your own or with a small group....See yourself walking around, looking for whatever birds or other animals you see. You look in the trees, in the bushes, up in the skies, and you notice all types of wildlife... You can take out your camera or use your binoculars to frame the image and see it more clearly.

Then, focus in on one particular bird and watch it fly through the air or move through the trees...Notice where it goes, the other birds it interacts with... Perhaps it swoops around looking for food... Perhaps it finds something and grabs it in its bill... Maybe it joins a group of other birds and they fly together...Whatever it does, just watch it move about...Then imagine that you are this bird, seeing things from that bird's eye view.

Now focus on an animal that lives on the ground and watch it move around...It might be a squirrel, a fox, a rabbit, a deer... Whatever it is, notice where it goes, what it does...Notice if it sees other animals or joins with them to look for food together... Then, notice some young animals... They may be with their mothers or running around and playing....Again, just notice what they do as they move about and play...Then imagine that you are one of these animals, seeing things from that animal's point of view.

Now imagine that you are on a hiking or camping trip with a small group, or go on your own. You have a backpack with equipment and food, maybe a small tent for an overnight stay... See yourself walking along the trail. Look around you as you walk. Pay attention to the different trees, plants, and animals you see.

Then, see yourself getting towards the end of your hike. You put down your backpack and gear and take some time to relax. Perhaps you prepare a meal or have a snack you have brought with you. Then, as you relax, you look around at your environment and notice any birds and other animals around you. You feel very comfortable, very relaxed. You feel like you are a part of nature and feel very much at peace. Later you can always come back to this spot in your imagination to feel that sense of relaxation and peace and being part of nature.

Now imagine that you are walking around your neighborhood, noticing the trees, plants, flowers, and any animals that are there. Then, you walk or drive to a nearby park, and you continue your walk there.

Now you are in a field or garden full of flowering plants. Just go around and look at the leaves or flowers. Take some time to touch them and smell them. Notice any sounds that you hear. Perhaps you notice a small bird, like a hummingbird or swallow, fly by and alight on a branch. Possibly a small squirrel or rabbit runs by. Or maybe you notice some spiders, beetles, ants, or other insects. Just take some time to look around and notice what's there.

Finally, imagine that you are playing a game like paintball or lasertag in the woods. You are on a small team, and you are holding your paintball or laser gun, as you look around for members of the other team to aim at. At the same time, you try to evade their shots by ducking or hiding behind trees and bushes so they can't see you. So go on and playfully run around the woods, and feel like a kid again as you play. You feel joyful, excited, as you race around.

So now, feeling this sense of joy and excitement and feeling very relaxed and peaceful, come back to the present. I'm going to count backwards from 5 to 1, and as I do, you'll come back into the room. Five, four – coming back now. Three, two, almost back. And one. You are back in the room. So open your eyes, feeling very good.

Later, take some time to write down some of these ideas for getting more work or expanding your business and think about how to put them into action.

Chapter 7: Improving the Environment Around You

Since there has been growing concern about the increasing toxicity in our environment and what to do about it, this chapter discusses how you might improve your own environment at home and at work.

Becoming Conscious of What Needs Changing

A first step is becoming conscious of what may be wrong with your current living and work space, and then consider what changes you can make.

I became much more aware of what's wrong and what to change after living part-time in L.A. for two years. I spent about 2-3 weeks in L.A. and Oakland, and drove back and forth once a month. At first this was a grand adventure, a great change of scene, which I began to get involved in the film business in L.A. But during my last two months there, I began to feel more and more oppressed by the environment, and more appreciative of the much more eco-friendly area where I live in Oakland.

The crowded streets and freeways in L.A. especially began to feel oppressive. The two buildings I lived in – one a secure apartment building, the other a townhouse -- both had enclosed parking. It was like a haven for my car when I got home. But when I left the building, most of the time I was almost immediately thrust into a traffic jam, packed with trucks, SUVs, and buses, as well as cars. There was a pervasive sound of honking, squealing tires, and occasional yells. So no wonder people putting on events usually allowed about 30 extra minutes to an hour for people to arrive, because the traffic was so all pervasive and unpredictable.

One way that I and other Angelinos learned to deal with all this traffic was to reduce our travel around the city beyond 10 to 15 miles away. Or we would adjust our travel schedules to go to events in the middle of the day from about 10 to 2 or in the evening after 7:30 or 8 p.m. when there was less traffic. Increasingly, I found that many people set up meetings using video cams, Skype, or phone conferences, so no one had to travel at all. It's as if technology had come along to help us deal with the growing problem of more and more cars on the road. In turn, one thing I really appreciated in coming back to the Bay Area was the much reduced traffic, so I felt freer to go to events all over the area at different times of the day, rather than retreating due to oppressive traffic.

So what would you like to change and improve in your own environment? One way to get started is to do an environmental assessment at home and at work, to see what things in your environment bother you the most. Then, think about how you might change them or what you can do, so you will feel less bothered by them.

How to Fix Up Your Environment at Home

One way to fix up your environment at home is to take a walk around your house and notice what's wrong. You can do this individually, with your partner, with a friend, or with a handyman or environmental consultant. Possibly there may be cracks in the walls or around the windows, often due to the earth settling or heavily rainfalls, and these might be patched. Also, look for leaky faucets or pipes. Check your electrical outlets to see that they are still working effectively. Look at your fuse boxes and consider if the fuses are powerful enough to carry an increased electric lode if you have a lot of high-tech devices. Or if not, consider upgrading to a breakers system, which will provide you more power and will quickly shut-off when there is a strain on the system.

Another approach is to look at your house using feng shui techniques or work with a feng shui consultant. By doing so, you may find things that should be rearranged or repositioned in line with feng shui principles, which are designed to promote a smooth flow of energy in your environment. For instance, if you have furniture blocking doorways, this could be blocking the free flow of energy in the house.

You might also consider what you can get rid of to free up space in your house. Organizational consultants call this the "purge" stage, and they recommend doing this in the beginning of organizing your work and personal life, so you eliminate what you don't need.

I once belonged to the chapter of a business referral group – BNI -- that had an organizational consultant as a member. When we had a one-on-one meeting, she looked around my house to see what she might organize. The first thing she told me to do was to go through my house and get rid of unnecessary papers and files. How to determine if they were unnecessary? She suggested getting rid of anything I hadn't looked at in over two or three years. She recommended doing the same for clearing out my clothes closet and drawers.

Well, that was about 6 years ago, and I found it difficult to stay on task, since one of the things I least like doing is going through old files and papers. It would probably be easier to throw out the whole pile that had accumulated for several years – but once I start going through it, I start wondering whether I will use something again or not. And as a writer, sometimes I have found a use for things I have kept for years without looking at them during this time, though probably I could have found another source for this information had I discarded this material. So, a little like the addict who keeps returning to rehab, I'm determined to try again, particularly since I have collected even more papers and files since I first tried to get rid of things, and I'm sure most are unnecessary to keep, too.

So what can you get rid of? Take some time to go through your house with a garbage can or large paper bag by your side, and perhaps for added support have a friend, partner, or organizational consultant accompany you. Then, if you haven't used something for years and don't think you will use it again in the near future, toss it out. Afterwards, reward yourself for clearing out all of this extra space in your life.

Another way to spark up your home environment is to look at the art pieces you have on your walls or on your desks, tables, or shelves. If you still like them, great! But sometimes you may no longer like a piece or feel that it is out of synch with other art pieces or the overall look of your place. You may even find that a piece seems too negative now that you want to create a more positive feel for your environment, such as if you have a painting that shows a wrong in society or a suffering victim. Whatever the reason, if you no longer like the piece or it doesn't fit in now, get rid of it, too.

Conversely, you may find some empty spaces that might benefit from art work to perk up your walls or furniture. If so, get some paintings, photographs, or sculptures you like -- or create them yourself. In choosing what to display, look for art that feels positive and upbeat to help create a comfortable, positive place. Avoid images that show conflict, suffering, or sadness. They may be important pieces and great to look at in museums and art galleries. But having them around your house can bring you down.

Another way to perk up your home is to add some humorous art pieces or toys that will make you and others smile when you look at them. For instance, I found a few colorful squeezy balls and a squiggly purple worm with big black eyes which I plunked on top of two couches. Soon I found that guests who sit on these couches commonly start squeezing the ball or the worm. And they are even more intrigued when the worm suddenly glows because it has been tapped or shaken in a certain way. You can find similar objects at a local toy store, gift store, garage sale, or thrift store.

You might also collect fun objects that express who you are. For example, some people have collections of unicorns, penguins, toy dogs, model cars, or other objects on display around their house or in a special cabinet or book shelf.

Then, too, try adding more plants to your house – from potted plants to flowers from your garden or local florist.

Vision boards are another way to make your environment more appealing. To create a vision board, find some images that represent goals or personal characteristics you would like to have in your life. You can easily find some images by going through old magazines like *People* and *Home and Gardens,* and cutting them out. Then, glue or tape them to a large art board – one that about 14"x17" or 16"x20." While most boards I've seen use a white background, you can use any color. After you create your board, post it where you can easily see it, like on a bulletin board in your bedroom, office, or kitchen. Then, make it a point to look at your vision board each day to remind yourself of these characteristics or goals you want to attain.

Still another way to enhance your environment is by putting in a fish tank with different types of small fish and creating an attractive environment in the tank for them to swim through, such as gently flowing sea grass and pieces of coral.

Consider ways to improve your lighting, too. For instance, use a dimmer switch, so you have bright lighting where you want it, but at times, you can dim the lights or set up colored lighting to create a special mood.

Pay attention to the sounds in your home, as well. Take some time to listen and notice what you hear. Are there sounds outside that you don't like? Consider soundproofing to keep them out, or play soft music to cover them up. Possibly use music and sound effects to set the mood, such as by playing upbeat, lively music to energize you and playing slow, soft music to calm you down.

Even smells might contribute to your environment, such as using incense or flowers to help you feel more cheerful or more relaxed.

Organizing your environment so it is neat and cleaned regularly will help, too. And try taking occasional walks around your house and yard or around communal areas in your apartment or condo. As you walk, look for other things you can do to create a more pleasant environment, too.

In short, there are all sorts of ways to improve your environment at home.

How to Fix Up Your Environment at Work

While you are more limited in what you can do at work, you may still be able to make some beneficial changes. For example, perk up your desk with humorous or beautiful objects or art pieces. Put objects around you that relate to your personality or look, such as one woman banker who loves purple did by surrounding herself with all sorts of purple objects, such as purple cars, dolls, and flowers.

Another suggestion for work is to add uplifting photos and paintings on the walls of your office or cubicle. Or contribute such photos and paintings to a communal room to be shared by all.

As you consider the possibilities, you'll come up with many different things you can do to create a better environment both at home and at work.

Part 5: Building Your Creativity and Brain Power

Chapter 8: Becoming More Creative and Innovative

Since the essence of creativity lies in coming up with new ideas, doing things differently, and thinking of alternative approaches, you can develop that ability like any other skill. Then, you can use that ability to come up with more ideas for new products and services, for new business ventures, for new ways of organizing group activities, and for better ways of responding to change.

Your creativity is most effective when channeled to respond to a significant need and organized to lead to a productive outcome. As the Kaiser Aluminum motto goes: "Find a need and fill it."

If you have a particular project, question, or problem to solve, you can directly focus your creative abilities towards that end. Don't just think, "I want to become more creative," but direct your creativity to a particular task. Your creativity expands when you perform acts that trigger your creative thinking and imagination.

The following mental imagery techniques can help you further develop the qualities that make up creativity – the ability to perceive and think in innovative ways and an openness to alternative ways of doing things. These techniques will limber up your mental thinking. Then, you can apply this outlook to any area in which you choose to express your creativity.

Ways to Develop Your Creativity

Three key ways to develop your creative abilities are these. One, see new uses for things. Two, find new methods or materials to attain a goal. Three, make changes in what exists or combine what exists in new ways. The more you develop your abilities in these areas, the more creative you become, and the more you can direct your creativity to be more effective in your work, business, or personal life.

- Discover New Uses for Things

Discovering new uses for things is a good way to gain maximum productivity for whatever you have at less cost. You need less, because you can do more with what you have. As such, you increase the value of what you have, such as when you find new uses for a tool or piece of equipment. Similarly, you can reduce expenses by using items you have for other purposes. Or if you market this product, you can expand this market by thinking of different ways people can use it. Or maybe you can solve a problem by using something in a new way. Finding new uses for something can even turn into big sales.

A good example is the Pet Rock craze from about 20 years ago. The designer took a simple stone, packaged it in a fancy box, called it a Pet Rock, and sales zoomed. Another example of a new use turning into something successful is the creation of the Post-It note, which you'll find in dozens of shapes, sizes, and colors in stores today. Originally, the Pet Rock was developed by the 3M Company after the research people came up with the wrong glue formula and the glue wasn't strong enough. But one employee found he could use the weak glue on a piece of paper to mark a hymnal in church, and that led the company to come up with new ways to use that glue for temporary uses – which became a multi-million dollar business.

So now that you see the benefits of thinking of new uses for something, try practicing yourself.

Begin by seeing how many new and unusual uses you can create for familiar items to get your creative juices flowing. Then, apply the process to a specific situation, such as at work, where you really do want to discover new uses for things. Try this technique alone or brainstorm with a friend, associate, or work group. Write down the items you are brainstorming about and note all the different uses you come up with.

To trigger your imagination, look around your office or house and jot down the names of the objects you see. Now for each object, write down as many uses as you can, making them as novel as possible. Feel free to change the size, shape, or color of the object. Or combine two or more objects and think of uses for them together.

For example, what can you do with a paper clip? You might bend it, stretch it, twist it around into different shapes. Then, once it has been changed, think about how you or anyone else might use it? For instance, if you were a chimpanzee, you could use that clip to dig for termites in a log. You could twist it in a lock on a door to get out of the house. Or if you were an artist, you could use the clip to scratch a picture in the sand. Or suppose you were a teenager doing decorations for a dance. You could string paper clips together to create a chain to dangle from the walls. In short, let your mind go as you think of the many possibilities.

Now imagine that you have two different types of objects. For instance, what can you do with a piece of paper and a chair? A newspaper and a cup? A stapler and a picture hook? Just think of any two objects and imagine what you might do with them.

Once you feel warmed up, think about any situation where you might apply this technique. For example, if your company is marketing a new product, think of all the possible uses for this product or all the ways the company might advertise it. Whatever your work or personal situation, think how you might use what you have in other different and useful ways. Later, you can select the good ideas and put them to use.

- <u>Using New Methods or Materials to Achieve a Goal</u>

Using new methods or materials to achieve a goal can often be just what you need when you can't get to a goal the way you planned. These new methods or materials might also provide a cheaper, more effective way to get to your goal, such as sending e-mails rather than writing a letter on paper and mailing it through the post office. As the famous motto states: "Necessity is the mother of invention." If you need to get someplace and don't have what you need to get there, your ingenuity can help you find another way.

For instance, suppose you want to be hired for a particular job. You know you can do it, but the requirements ask for credentials or experience you don't have. If you want the job badly enough, come up with other ways to get it, so you shine by showing how innovative you are. For instance, put together a plan showing where the company is going over the next few years and how you can help the company get there. Or perhaps complete a small part of a pending project on your own and do it well. Or at the interview, talk about your future vision for your job and the company. The result: by thinking ahead and creatively, you can show the people doing the hiring that some of their requirements aren't necessary. You have shown through your creativity that you can do the job better than anyone else.

Meanwhile, as you seek new methods or materials to achieve a goal, think, "I can do it" and keep that "can-do" attitude in mind when you put these new methods and materials into practice. By approaching any goal, no matter how hard it may seem to achieve, with this "can do" approach you are more likely to achieve it. Just remind yourself, "I can do it," and say the words to yourself. It also helps to think of an image that conveys this "can do" attitude to you, such as a brightly colored balloon that lifts you up as a reminder you can continually rise to even greater heights. Also, it helps to have an image of yourself achieving the desired result.

A good way to set goals is to think creatively about how to respond to future trends in your field. To do so, stay up with current developments and project them ahead 6 months to a year in the future. Then, imagine how you might respond to these trends. Think about new ways to use what you already have (such as applying your skills in different ways). Or imagine new methods or materials you can use (such as what new skills, products, or services you can offer).

A good tool to limber up your thinking is brainstorming to come up with ideas. Begin by thinking of a goal, need, or want. Then, see how many ways you can think of to achieve that goal or fill that need or want. Brainstorm with a friend or associate if you wish.

To start the brainstorming process, make a short list of activities you'd like to see handled another way, such as commuting to work or redesigning a procedure in your company. Then, taking each activity individually, write down as many new approaches as you can, making them as novel as possible. Imagine you have unlimited resources to create solutions, and let your ideas come as quickly as possible. Later you can evaluate these new ideas and choose any you can use.

• Changing What Is to What You Want

Changing what exists or combining what exists in new ways is a way to use familiar objects or people to create unique arrangements or organizations. This change or combining things technique is especially good for inventing new products and services, reorganizing a group of people, or creating a decorative scheme for your office or home.

To begin, think of two or three familiar objects or people and write them down. Have some overall goal in mind, such as creating a new product or a more effective work group. Or you can work on brainstorming new ideas to get your creative juices flowing and apply this approach to practical situations later.

Now imagine a scene with these two or three objects or people. If you have a specific purpose in mind, use that to set the scene, such as imagining the people at work doing their everyday jobs when they begin to work with the selected objects. Alternatively, make your scene as wild and fantastic as you wish to stimulate your creative processes, such as imagining everyone in a "Survivor-like" island setting or a futuristic city where all things are possible. You can also make these objects or people larger or smaller than normal.

For instance, say you choose some Coke bottles, a sink, and some sponges. As you look at the bottles, you might imagine them as part of a futuristic city where the streets are paved with dishes and the houses are shaped like bottles. Or maybe turn the sink and sponges into a harbor with boats. Let your imagination range completely free, and if you wish, draw a picture of your vision.

Alternatively, if you are seeking a practical result, such as a new product, you might consider how these two or three objects could be used to create that. For instance, maybe the sponge could be placed around the middle of a bottle to create a floating bottle, so people could take their drinks into the pool without losing them.

Whatever your purpose, let your inner creativity go where it will without trying to censor or edit it in this first stage of coming up with ideas. Wait until later to critique and evaluate any ideas you come up with.

Chapter 9: Improving Your Memory

Improving your memory can increase your success in work and business in numerous ways. This chapter describes the ways you can apply your better memory and techniques for achieving these gains in memory power.

The Advantages of a Good Memory

Improving your memory can help you better remember tasks, so you don't forget to accomplish anything essential. If you keep lists, a better memory can help you recall the details you weren't able to write down.

Also, a good memory can help at cocktail parties and business networking mixers. By remembering people, you increase your chances of getting jobs and clients. And if people offer referrals, your memory can help you keep track of these contacts and what to say to them, though make notes on all the business cards you collect to jog your memory later.

Then, too, a better memory can help you give a more polished presentation or speech, tell jokes and stories that make you more interesting, and recall specific prices and offers to get a better deal. You can think of dozens of other benefits.

In turn, using mental imagery techniques can help train your memory. For example, one man used to have trouble remembering the names of people he met at cocktail and business networking parties. But then he began concentrating on getting an associated image for everyone he met based on some feature that stood out, such as an unusual name, striking physical feature, or noteworthy article of clothing. Now he found the introductions stayed with him, especially since he turned the process into a networking game. The more names he remembered from the business cards he collected, the higher his score. One reason he did so well is because creating an image made him pay more attention when he was introduced. Secondly, the image made the person stand out in some way.

Memory Training Exercises

Here are some memory training exercises to help you improve your memory in three key ways:

• You increase your ability to focus on what you want to remember.

• You work on making a clear memory picture; then file it in your mind for later recall.

• You use your powers of visualization and meditation to retrieve a memory.

• Improving Your Ability to Focus

Your ability to focus is a key memory tool, because many people have trouble remembering because they don't make a clear picture of what they want to remember. They don't pay enough attention in the beginning.

Naturally, you can remember all sorts of things without being attentive, since we unconsciously absorb information all the time and much of this stays with us, even if we are unaware of it. But, this casual absorption of information can be a hit or miss proposition.

Thus, when you're in a situation where it's particularly important to remember something, learn to pay close attention by using a memory trigger. This trigger can be almost any type of gesture or physical sign—such as bringing your thumb and forefinger together or raising your thumb. Whatever signal you use, it's designed to remind you to be especially alert and listen or watch closely, so you'll remember all you can.

To create this trigger, get relaxed, perhaps close your eyes, and choose the sign you want to use. Then, make this gesture and as you do, think to yourself: "I will pay attention now. I will be very alert and aware, and I will lock this information in my memory, so I can recall it later."

Do this trigger creation process several times, and later that day or the next day, practice using this trigger in some real-life situations. Find at least three times when you're especially interested in remembering something, and use your trigger to make yourself more alert. As you make this gesture, repeat the same words to yourself as in your concentration exercises: "I will pay attention now. I will be very alert and aware, and I will lock this information in my memory, so I can recall it later."

Repeat both parts of this exercise (the meditation and the real-life practice) for a week to condition yourself to associate the action you want to perform (paying attention) with the trigger (raising your thumb). Once this association is locked in, you don't need to continue practicing the exercise, as long as you continue regularly to use the trigger.

Then, any time you're in a situation where you want to pay especially careful attention, use your trigger, and automatically you'll become more attentive and alert.

• Making a Clear Memory Picture

Besides paying attention, having a good memory depends on making a clear and sharp mental picture or recording of the person, place, or event you want to remember. Often we don't make this picture or recording very well. As a result, we may think we remember what we have seen, but we don't. Courtroom witnesses, for example, often recall an event inaccurately, although they may be positive they are correct.

Accordingly, before you can recall something properly, you must have a clear impression of it in the first place. One way to do this is to think of yourself as a camera or audio recorder, taking in completely accurate pictures or recordings of what you experience. Then, as you observe and listen, make your impressions like pictures or tape recordings in your mind.

To practice seeing, observe some object, person, event, or setting and imagine yourself as a camera taking this picture. Take some time to really observe as you get it in focus. Then, turn away from what you are observing and recall what you can. Perhaps write down what you recall. Finally, look back and ask yourself: "How much did I remember? What did I forget? What did I recall that wasn't there?"

To practice listening, imagine you are a tape, cassette, or video recorder, and you are listening to the playback. Listen very closely, paying full attention. Then, turn off the recorder and recall what you can.

As you practice with these methods, after a while, you'll automatically start making more accurate memory pictures or recordings in your mind.

An ideal way to use these techniques is with a mental awareness trigger. Then, whenever you use that trigger, you'll immediately imagine yourself as a camera or recorder and firmly impress that scene on your mind for later recall.

• <u>Using Your Power of Visualization to Recall an Image</u>

After you have done all you can to register a memory impression, the final step is doing everything you can to recall it. Even if you think you have forgotten, these memory techniques will help you release your unconscious processes, so you can dig back into your inner storage area in your unconscious to retrieve it.

To help you recover a name, phone number, location of an object, route you traveled, or anything else, recreate the original experience in your mind as realistically and dramatically as possible. Imagine that you have a large picture screen before and focus on that. If you can replay the experience in reality, do it, to recapture the memory. A good example is when you don't remember where you parked your car. You can focus on mentally replaying the route you walked from the car to your destination. Then, like a camera operator, rewind the tape and mentally play it backwards until you get to your car.

Similarly, use a dramatic visualization to recall a name. Visualize the person before you. Imagine that you are meeting for the first time. Pay careful attention to who else is there and the setting. Make your picture as complete as possible. Then, greet this person as you did when you first met, and listen carefully as this person tells you his or her name.

To recall a phone number, visualize a phone before you and see the person you are going to call near a phone, awaiting your call. Now go to wherever you keep your phone numbers and open your phone book to this person's name. Or if you have recently written down the number, visualize writing it down as the person tells you his or her number.

Or suppose you want to recall where you put some object, such as your keys. Think back to the last time you had that object. Where were you? What were you doing with it? Visualize yourself using that object. Then, when you are finished with it, observe what you do with it to put it away.

To help you recall an event, imagine yourself in the situation as vividly as possible. Notice the setting, the buildings, the people around you. Imagine you are a movie director and this is a scene that is about to unfold before you. You hold the script in your hands, and at your cue, the actors begin to play out the scene. You notice everything, hear everything they say. If you want to move ahead faster in the scene, simply turn a page of your script, say "cut," and direct the actors to start again in a later scene.

Once you have gained practice in recalling the memories you want with these techniques, feel free to develop your own imagery to help you recall anything. For example, see yourself as an investigative reporter covering a story rather than being a movie director filming a script. The key to recall is to imagine yourself as vividly as possible in the situation you want to remember. Then, use your mental picture or recording of that situation to stimulate your memory of the original event.

Part 6: Building Better Relationships

Chapter 10: Improving Your Relationships at Home and at Work

Since conflict is a growing problem in relationships at home and at work, this chapter focuses on ways to improve your own relationships in your personal life and in your work and business.

Using Your Intuitive Abilities to Gain Accurate Insights into Others

One key way to have better relationships is to become more aware of your inner intuitive voice and use it to better understand and assess others. By understanding others better, you can improve your ability to relate to them and up your chances for success. Our intuition often gives us insights into people that, if we are aware of them, can guide our reactions to them.

Today, this intuitive awareness can be especially helpful because of the huge number of scammers in today's fast-paced competitive world, where the potential for anonymity and the Internet provides a handy cover. Commonly, people go on first impressions, which can be misleading.

These impressions can be misleading because often, we don't recognize the cues we are picking up from others. Though the mind registers what we are sensing, we are not consciously aware of these cues, because the mind is trying to protect us from sensory overload.

But this protective process can also block us from recognizing things we should be aware of, such as the little twinge of caution that tells us someone isn't telling the truth or is setting a trap for us. As a result, problems can arise from missed signals.

Conversely, we can miss a great opportunity because we don't see it, act on it, or don't trust the insight we are getting. In addition, this lack of awareness can lead us to overlook the signals that let us know that someone is hurt or angry at something we are saying or doing, which can lead to conflict. And, sometimes, we may not really want to acknowledge that something is true; because the truth is so painful. We want to deny it or delay hearing it, so we block it.

Failing to recognize and act on these inner cues can sometimes be disastrous in both a personal or business relationship. So it's essential to recognize a problem quickly to avoid or minimize the result.

Let me give you an example. I'll call them Dave and Norma. They lost a lot of money in an investment scam for a new business, because they didn't to notice the warning signals telling them to stay away, after their friends invited them to a presentation of a new direct-sales program for health products. Instead, they were taken in by the founder's verbal assurances of the high earnings possible and his smooth self-assured appearance of success. At the same time, they ignored the warning signals that cautioned them to "check it out," such as the little twinges of confusion and uncertainty they felt. So they signed in, investing about $5000. But the promised advertising and support never materialized and, after a few weeks, the founder disappeared, taking most of the money with him.

In another case, Cynthia got involved in with a smooth-talking con artist, Hank, who led her to believe in his strong love for her. He flattered her, seeming to show great interest in whatever she had to say, and he treated her to expensive dinners in trendy restaurants. But she failed to notice that when she asked him about himself, he spoke in generalities about his great success in different businesses around the US as an investor. He mentioned companies she never heard of, but she didn't think anything was wrong with that, since these were start-up businesses in other parts of the country. As a result, once she was passionately in love in Hank, Cynthia didn't notice or didn't want to notice the gradual changes he introduced in their relationship.

First, he wanted to spend more time at home with her, so they went out less and less. Then, he wanted her to wait for important calls from him at home when he was out of town. When he corrected her by asking her to wear something different or suggesting she answer the phone in a different way, she went along, thinking that his corrections showed his concern. He was just helping her become a better person, she thought. She didn't realize that Hank was increasingly isolating her from others and getting her to follow his commands.

As a result, when Hank asked her to borrow money for a new project, explaining that a check to him had been delayed and he would pay her back the next week when it arrived, Cynthia meekly said yes. She didn't want to anger or disappoint him. But after she gave him the money, Hank was oddly busy and unavailable to see her, and eventually he stopped calling. When she called him to find out what was wrong, she discovered his phone was disconnected. It was the classic scam of getting someone to trust and believe, and then taking something valuable from them.

The desire to believe can be very strong. It can cloud our inner perceptions. Even someone who is normally very perceptive and intuitive about people and situations can be sucked in. Professional con artists know this, and they use this desire to believe to persuade people to trust them. However, if you listen to your inner voice or vision as well as to your reason, you will be better able to assess people and won't fall for such scams.

The Danger Signals to Watch for in Relationships

So what should you look for? These danger signals come in two forms.

First, you may get <u>an initially intense warning</u> in the form of an inner voice, image, strange tingling sensation, or gut-level feeling. It'll be telling you that things aren't quite what they seem or the person telling you something isn't to be trusted;

Second, you may get <u>a less intense but recurring warning</u> in the same form. Don't ignore this signal. Instead, ask yourself if things are as they seem, and proceed with caution as you investigate further to see if your warning signal is correct. If you're in touch with your intuition, you will usually find it is.

So the first step is thus to pay attention. Notice any inner-warning signals you experience, however they come to you—voices, images, or gut-level feelings.

Next, investigate the warning—ask questions, get supporting information, and seek explanations of things you don't understand or things that seem vague or contradictory. Verify assumptions.

Also, ask yourself why you trust someone or believe something is true. Look for underlying reasons and motivations, which might be clouding your ability to assess the situation. Try to look behind surface appearances—such as the seeming professionalism or slickness of the person who is trying to persuade you to do something—to get the inner truth.

Additionally, pay attention to external warnings that echo your internal warnings. Or if you get external warnings first, look within to see if these warnings trigger your own inner warning signal.

Then, tune into your inner knowing and put aside your desired beliefs to discover what this knowing part of you really thinks.

While many of these suggestions may seem obvious, often we are so busy that we don't have the time or energy to check every detail personally. Instead, we trust what people tell us and what friends recommend. Sometimes we so strongly want what we hear to be true that we eagerly embrace it and the people who tell us the information, and we tune out those who caution us against it.

That's why the inner-warning signal is so important. It's a kind of defense, advising us when to pay extra attention to something, because we unconsciously or intuitively sense that something isn't quite right. This sense could be wrong, but it's important to pay attention to it, because it usually picks up cues we don't consciously notice, and these cues are a signal there could be problems ahead.

Remember that outer appearances can lead to overlooking the warnings of your inner insight. For example, people conveying the image of success and knowledge often convince others to do things based on this image, even when there is nothing to support this. Their outer appearance is powerful enough to overcome any warning signals people may have, especially when one sees other people who are convince by this image to believe what this person says.

Thus, it is important to put aside external appearances, especially when you get repeated warning signals that things aren't right. Look more closely at what's behind that outer shell.

For example, one woman I'll call Debbie met a promoter who wanted to start a travel club. He talked about how she was the perfect person to help organize the club. She would get an excellent salary, be on the executive board; have travel privileges; and enjoy many other benefits. He talked convincingly and asked Debbie to do some preliminary work for him on a deferred salary, while he waited for funds from a stock issue to come through.

But as they talked, Debbie's inner radar began picking up some danger signals. She experienced a knotted up feeling in her stomach, and she saw the image of a black raven warning her to watch out. As a result, she calmly told the man she would have to think about his proposal and asked him to leave his business plan. When she did some checking, she learned he was operating his business out of his bedroom; he only had promises of backing; and there was no stock issue. Also, she discovered that several other people who had worked for him on spec had ended up with nothing. So she avoided being sucked into his scheme.

Thus, if you know when to trust your inner knowing or gut feelings, you can make better choices about people. Consider any warning signal to be your inner radar that tells you to look further or proceed with caution. Your intuition is not always 100% -- it's more like a yellow flashing light that urges you to look both ways before crossing, because it may or may not be safe. Then, if the crossing looks all clear, that's a sign to move ahead – in your personal or your work relationships.

You can increase the accuracy of your intuition, as you notice when it is correct and when it is more like telling you "maybe." The process is like looking through a magnifying glass, so you see what you want to learn about more clearly.

How Your Intuition Can Help You Learn About Others

Your intuition can help you learn about someone in three ways:

1) It'll help you get a quick accurate and clear first impression when you meet someone new. Notice any words, images, or thoughts that come to mind, and notice what they mean to you. For instance, if the image of a playful kitten comes to mind, that suggests someone who is warm, friendly, and spontaneous. If you see an image of a fox, that person might be aggressive, cunning, and clever. Interpret the images by what they mean to you. Later check this impression from time to

time to see if it is still accurate. You could have made an error, or the person may have changed.

2) It'll help you get an advance impression when you set up a meeting with someone, so you can have a better first meeting, though again be flexible in order to adapt as necessary when you meet. Visualize the person you plan to meet with in your mind's eye, and see yourself having this meeting. Notice what you pick up about the person, and imagine how you will respond. This process will help in prepping you for the real meeting.

3) It'll help you gain a more in-depth understanding of a person, so you can communicate and interact better or give that person useful advice. For example, as you talk to someone, notice what words, images, or thoughts come to mind, and notice what they tell you about the person. Then, use these insights to better respond to that person so you match that person's style or act as a compliment to it. Say you are with someone who is warm and friendly; you might be more warm and friendly yourself. Or if you are with someone who is guarded and shy, you might give that person more space to trust and feel comfortable with you; then he or she will be willing to share more.

So try paying more attention to your intuition and what it's telling you to help you in building your relationships and know which ones to develop.

Chapter 11: Making Commitments, Betrayals, and Forgiveness

Since betrayals have been recently in the news, especially with the revelations about Tiger Woods, I'd like to talk about the importance of making and keeping commitments, betrayals, and forgiveness.

Making and keeping commitments is critical to the functioning of all levels of society – from commitments to oneself and one's personal relationships to business and society as a whole. Commitments are critical, because people depend on promises, agreements, contracts, treaties, and all other types of commitments to make choices and work together harmoniously. This trust is like a glue that keeps people and society together; it keeps businesses going. When commitments fail because someone doesn't keep an agreement or betrays a trust, there is an upheaval in that relationship. The result can be a broken friendship, a destroyed marriage, a conflict between business partners, a war between nations. You name it. When commitments are not kept, when trust is lost, all types of havoc can ensue.

The Tension Between Keeping and Breaking Commitments

Ironically, though, there is frequently a tension between keeping a commitment and breaking it, say by cheating in a relationship or eluding an agreement because a better opportunity comes along. The reason for the tension is the lure of a better short term opportunity or payoff versus the long term gain from keeping the commitment. As a result, as long as one isn't caught, the gain of breaking the commitment can outweigh the risk of getting found out. And often that gamble pays off. The lies, excuses, and explanations enable one to enjoy the undeserved or ill-gotten gains. So the likelihood of getting with the breach of trust is a reason to take the chance. But if the cover-up unravels, those affected by the failed commitment can feel betrayed – and relationships can be upended – though there is often a possibility of repairing the breach and gaining forgiveness.

This familiar scenario is played out again and again. Agreements are made with high hopes but are often broken, with varying consequences.

For example, you make a commitment to yourself to lose weight, and you promise yourself you'll stay on your diet. Then a tempting dessert at a party lures you and you succumb. You gain the immediate pleasure of the great taste. But the downside is you are more easily tempted again. You also lose the momentum of your diet, and your weight goes up, while you feel guilty. So you promise yourself once again that you'll try to be good next time, and you punish yourself by eating less and exercising more to get your weight back down. But then, as dieters know all to well, the cycle repeats itself again and again. Commitment, betrayal, guilt, and re-commitment, again and again.

Relationships are often affected by this same cycle. You begin most relationships with expectations of honesty, trust, and faithfulness, which may be sincerely made at the time. But then each partner may face many temptations to break these agreements and seek ways to cover up if they give in. However, like Tiger Wood's late night car crash, such cover-ups can unexpectedly be exposed, resulting in all sorts of losses. For instance, in Tiger's case, the small fine and payment for repairing the car is only the beginning. His reputation and marriage are on shaky ground, too. A key reason is that Tiger has long had a squeaky-clean image of propriety in the press; but now his affairs with three or more women are the subject of tabloid revelation and speculation. He has had to renegotiate a prenup and maybe make payments of millions of dollars to his wife to stay with him. He has paid at least one of the women he had an affair with a million or more to not reveal any more about their relationship to the press or in a book. He might lose endorsement contracts worth millions because of the damage to his clean-living image. And there's the loss of his cherished privacy, as the tabloids and other media explore every facet of his life.

But Tiger's story is just another example, though writ large, of what happens in relationships all the time. We promise to be loyal and true, and that's the accepted ideal. But then more often than not, someone cheats or appears to – and the battle to regain trust is on.

This same kind of promise, breach, and repair scenario plays out again and again in even everyday mundane situations. For instance, you say you will go to an event, but then you don't because something else comes up – and you don't call or write to cancel. You promise to carry out some action for someone, but then you forget. Often such everyday failures to keep commitments are overlooked. But if you break your commitments enough, you'll get a reputation of being unreliable, and you may not get invitations or requests again. You may find that others talk about you as someone who can't be trusted, and you may lose a friend or promotion, because someone feels they can't count on you.

The Negative Consequences of
Not Keeping Commitments

In short, there may be many reasons to fail to keep a commitment – from preferring to do something else to gaining a better opportunity to forgetting a commitment you made. But there can be many negative consequences, when others depend on you for something but you don't do it. Or they may feel betrayed when they find out you did something that violated their trust. Then, you have to make repairs if you can – but in many cases the repairs will be far more costly than if you kept your commitments in the first place. And in some cases, you won't be able to make repairs at all, because those affected regard the breach of trust so seriously, that they won't easily forgive you – now or at all.

For example, one woman I'll call Suzanne felt betrayed and was reluctant to forgive, when Marvin, a contractor she hired through a network of friends, charged her much more than she expected for a job. She met him when she joined a business referral group, and after they met to learn about each other's businesses, she mentioned a problem with a stuck door, and he agreed to fix it, as well as some other things in her house. He told Suzanne he worked on an hourly basis and just had to bring a few hinges which might cost about $20 to quickly fix the door. Then, he gave Suzanne a flyer listing his skills and hourly rate.

So Suzanne hired Marvin, and a couple of days later, he arrived and in about 10 minutes fixed her door and offered to fix her other house problems the following week. But when Suzanne suggested combining the cost of this short project with that of the larger job planned for next week, Marvin said no. He claimed he had a two hour minimum and this was a separate project, so she needed to pay him now, as well as give him the money for the hinges, which he charged at three times their retail price, because he had bought the hinges for her.

Suzanne was furious, since Marvin had never mentioned the minimum before and his literature said nothing about it. Worse, she felt intimidated by Marvin's determined look, as he waited for her to pay him then and there. So she paid. Though she didn't let on that anything was wrong, she felt cheated by Marvin's actions. As a result, she not only cancelled the job planned the following week, but she never hired him to do anything else and she no longer spoke to him at the group's meetings. Of course, she never gave him any referrals, and she told the group's president about what he did. So Marvin was put on notice that if he tried anything like that again with another member, he would be out of the group.

For many, a failure to keep a small commitment may not seem to matter, but it does. For example, I belong to and organize a number of groups through MeetUp, a Website where people can promote a variety of group activities and invite people to sign up to attend. Very often people sign-up but don't attend, although it is very easy to change a "yes" RSVP to a "no." When people don't show up, usually because something else came up, they may not think it's a big deal to change their RSVP. But it is, because they have betrayed a promise to do something that can have negative consequences for others and for them. For instance, the host may make preparations, even reservations, expecting a certain number of people to attend, but then they don't. And those who do come can be disappointed because of the smaller than expected turnout. Also, if the attendance is limited, a "yes" RSVP can keep someone on a waiting list from attending, because there seems to be no space, when there is. The "no show" can additionally lead to negative consequences for the person who doesn't show up, since some hosts have two or three strikes policies, so if someone fails to show up without canceling two or three times, they can't attend in the future.

There are also numerous examples of business losses and failures, resulting from someone who doesn't keep promises or commitments. A notorious example is the Bernie Madoff scandal; another is the Bay Bridge closure for repairs after a flawed part of a tower fell down, because someone didn't properly check for structural weaknesses on the bridge. And many everyday business screw-ups occur because someone didn't keep an agreement to do what they said or be where they said they would be. You can think of many more breakdowns due to failed promises and commitments in your own experiences.

Thus, only make those commitments and promises you believe you can keep. And should circumstances change, quickly let anyone depending on you know. Also, consider any commitments and promises you make to be binding, except for special circumstances, so you take breaking your commitments and promises quite seriously. Don't just regard them like something you can buy and easily take back for a full return. Even small commitments and promises lead people to depend on you, and if people can't, don't make those commitments and promises. Or make it clear when you aren't sure. Consider being unsure a little like an engagement to get married or an option period to consider whether to buy a house or a business. This way, you are clear where you stand, and others will appreciate for it. As the popular country song goes: "You've got to stand for something, and if you don't, you will surely fall."

Dealing with Betrayals and the Power of Forgiveness

So what should you do when others don't keep their commitments to you and you feel let down or betrayed. That's where forgiveness comes in. As I heard one man say to another in a parking lot: "Life goes on, so you've got to forgive." If you don't forgive, you can hold that anger, resentment, even hate in your heart, towards someone you feel failed to honor their commitments and betrayed your trust. Even if your anger is justified, those negative feelings can build up and eat away at you.

So as you can, learn to forgive and let go. This doesn't mean you should forget – for you may not want to continue a relationship with someone who is unreliable or has betrayed you in your business or personal life. But you should learn to release the emotional baggage associated with whatever they did. This way you can move on, without feeling the negative emotions from what happened continually pulling on you. Yes, you may well remember what occurred and use that to guide you in whether and how to deal with that person in the future.

But through the power of forgiveness, you can learn what you have learned from that negative experience and move on.

Part 7: Here's to Your Health and the Food You Eat

Chapter 12: Improving Your Health

Since health has been a growing concern, this chapter features ways you might improve your health. These techniques are designed to supplement whatever you are already doing to stay healthy – so continue to listen to your doctor or other health practitioner. Some of these techniques incorporate the power of visualization to get what you want – in this case, better health.

How Your Powers of Visualization Can Help Your Health

Your mind power or powers of visualization can help you feel better and chase away simple ailments, like a cold or sore throat. They can also help you break bad habits, such as smoking or overeating. Of course, if anything is seriously wrong, see a doctor and use your mind power abilities along with medical supervision. But for everyday problems, these techniques have proved helpful for numerous people.

For example, one man used to come down with frequent colds and sore throats, which kept him off the job, because he feared coming down with something worse. When he got the first sign of a cold—usually a tightness in his throat—he believed the cold was inevitable.

But then, he learned to use his mind powers to ward off these illnesses. He started taking action as soon as he felt the first symptom of a cold or sore throat coming on. He sat down in a chair in his living room, closed his eyes, visualized healing energy pouring into himself from the earth and air around him. Then, he saw this energy form into a bright white beam, which he directed at the pain in his throat or head. Meanwhile, he thought to himself: "You will remain healthy. You will not get a cold. Your sore throat will go away."

Over the next few days, he continued this visualization a few times a day, until he felt the danger of getting ill was past. The result was that most of the time he was able to avoid coming down with colds or sore throats. And the few times he came down with something, he noticed it was much less severe than usual.

In another case, a teacher, used these techniques to control her weight. She had been battling the problem for several years, trying one diet after another, without much success. She would lose a few pounds, start approaching her ideal weight, and then lose her commitment to stay on her diet. After about five years, she was close to giving up, when she heard about the value of mind power techniques.

After finding a quiet comfortable place in her house, she began meditating on the reason she was having so much trouble staying on a diet. "Why can't I keep my weight down?" she asked her unconscious. "You need a reminder," her inner voice replied, "and you need to find ways to reward yourself each day for being good." She continued to dialogue with this voice for a while, and finally it told her a program to follow for the next two weeks. She should meditate briefly twice a day and affirm to herself: "You don't need to eat so much. You can eat less and you won't feel hungry." She should concentrate on having certain types of foods in her diet, mainly liquids, vegetables, fruits, and a protein drink. And when she took a vitamin pill with her meal, she should remind herself she was on a diet and needed to exercise control. She started her diet the next day, and by the end of the week she was well on her way to losing the 20 pounds she wanted to lose.

In a third case, a woman used these techniques to recover quickly from an accident and get right back to work. She was in the middle of organizing her house and office to prepare for a move, when she slipped and fell so her head hit the side of her stereo speaker. She didn't feel much pain, so she didn't realize it was serious until she started noticing spatters of blood on the floor.

But rather than get upset and excited, she calmly she asked herself questions like: "What do I do now?" and listened to her answers. Meanwhile, she kept her major goal in mind—to take care of the situation as quickly as possible, so she could return to work and make an upcoming deadline.

The result of this inner dialogue was that she calmly lay down, held some tissue to her head, and visualized the blood vessels in her head constricting and the blood slowing down, and in a few minutes the bleeding stopped. Then, still calm, relaxed, and feeling no pain, she lay down for about fifteen minutes to ride out the initial shock reaction that made her feel woozy, and she concentrated on those feelings going away. Once they were gone, she calmly called the emergency room at the hospital, drove herself there, and when the doctors put in eleven stitches to close up the large gash in her forehead, she saw herself floating outside her body, looking down on the process. Meanwhile, she kept thinking about her goal—to get home and back to work as quickly as possible.

As a result, the procedure went very quickly. She experienced practically no pain, and about four hours after the accident, she was back at work. Within a few days, the stitches were removed, and after another week, it was like the accident never happened.

By contrast, for other people, accidents that could have been handled in a few hours precipitated major life crises, because of their reaction. For instance, after a teacher in her 50s slipped in her bedroom, slightly fractured her hip, and was put in a cast for a few weeks, she turned that accident into a major catastrophe because of her negative attitude. She exaggerated all sorts of fears, which led her to see herself as an invalid and feel suicidal, rather than focusing on quickly getting well. So she ended up in the hospital for several months.

Thus, when illnesses and accidents happen, you can use a positive attitude and mobilize your inner forces to quickly combat the problem. You'll feel much better and heal more quickly as a result. These visualization techniques can do this, because the vast majority of our illnesses have some mental or psychological basis.

For example, feeling stress is a mental response to some situation, and numerous illnesses and bad conditions develop in response to stress. Also, stress lowers our resistance to certain diseases, so we may come down with something, usually in that part of our body that is the weakest. For instance, after experiencing stress some people come down with a cold; some with stomach cramps; others with a headache. Thus, using any relaxation technique can help your health by reducing stress.

Our expectations also influence whether we stay well or get sick. For instance, if you're around someone with a cold or get chilled, you may expect consciously or unconsciously to catch something—and if you expect it, you often will get what you expect. However, you can counteract or reverse your expectations by setting up a mental shield before you encounter a situation that could cause problems or by using a mental cleansing process afterwards.

Helping Yourself Heal in Different Situations

Yet even with such precautions, sometimes we all get sick or feel the telltale symptoms that warn us we may be coming down with something, such as feeling dizzy or having a sore throat. In this case, you can send healing energy to the part of your body at risk, so you may be able to reverse the process—or make the ensuing illness less serious.

Then, if you do get ill, your mind powers can make you feel better while recovering and speed your recovery. You see yourself feeling better and affirm you are getting better, too.

Finally, you can use a visualization to do a routine body check, and if you notice any weak spots, you can send healing energy there to possibly avoid a subsequent illness or problem.

Following are some techniques you can use to improve your health and the healing process, though see a doctor if the condition persists. Adapt each approach to your own needs or apply the basic principles to create other visualizations for other health problems.

To get rid of stress, use your mind powers to direct yourself to relax. Use a calming image or use self-talk to tell yourself you are getting more and more relaxed. You can also put on soothing music, dim the lights, and go to a place in your house which you associate with being calm and relaxed.

You can protect yourself from exposure to an illness through visualization in two ways. One is to mentally shield yourself in advance if you are going to be in a place where someone is ill or shield yourself immediately on encountering this person.

Another way to protect yourself is to cleanse yourself mentally after being exposed if you don't have time to create your mental shield before your exposure. You can cleanse yourself while you are still with the person or soon after you have been exposed. Then, if you remain in the area of exposure, you can put up your mental shield after cleansing to continue your protection.

Besides protecting you from illness, these shielding and cleansing techniques can protect you from negative people and situations. Use the shield to fend off any negativity, and use the cleansing approach to clear away any negativity.

To use the shielding technique, visualize a shield of white light around yourself when you feel threatened by an illness or any negativity. See this shield radiating from the center of your head and surrounding you completely. This shield provides a ring of protection around you, so that if any germs or negative forces hit this shield, they bounce right off.

To use the cleansing technique, visualize yourself standing in a small room, surrounded by brilliant white light. Experience the light pouring down around you like purifying water. As it does, lift your hands and brush any impurities from all parts of your body, as if you were cleansing yourself in a shower. Then, when you feel clean, step out of the shower of light, feeling protected and refreshed.

When you first feel you are getting sick—such as experiencing the sore throat that appears before you come down with a cold—you can send healing energy to that affected part to possibly reverse the process of getting ill or make the illness less serious. You might visualize a radiant bubble of healing energy around you. Then, feel this beam of energy pouring into you, and direct it to your affected part. Now feel this healing warmth and energy flowing into that area and healing it, so you feel fine.

A good technique for getting rid of headaches is mentally zapping them with a laser beam. Just visualize a laser beam of light coming from your head and going into your headache. As the light streams in, the headache begins to shatter and dissolve. Then, when it is gone or feels better, turn off the laser and open your eyes.

To feel better and get better faster, focus your attention on getting well. In addition, you can have a dialogue with your inner self to find out if there is anything special you should do to speed your recovery. After you get relaxed and close your eyes, ask yourself: "What should I do to speed my recovery?" Then, listen to the answer, and ask more questions if you need to, so you get any instructions you need. Later, keep this advice in mind while you are recovering. Also, see yourself participating in your everyday activities and being completely well as you repeat to yourself: "I am well. I am well. I am well." or "I feel fine. I feel fine."

Finally, you can use visualization to discover if there are any weak spots in your body, and if so, where they are. Then, you can send healing energy to strengthen them, using the bubble technique. To check out your body, take a mental trip through your circulation system and cells. As you travel, notice you are in a single cell with thousands of transparent cells around you. As you travel, you will feel a sense of warmth, like being immersed in a warm bath. However, notice if there are any cool or hot spots, for this may signify an area of your body that needs attention. If so, you can later send healing energy to this part.

Chapter 13: Enjoying Your Food Even More

Finally, this chapter deals with ways to enjoy your food more wherever you are. These techniques can be especially helpful when you travel and experience all sorts of new foods. Many of these techniques incorporate the power of visualization to make your eating experience more interesting.

Becoming More Aware of What You Are Eating

First, become more aware of what you are eating.

If the foods you are eating are a combination of ingredients, find out the individual ingredients. Then, see if you can distinguish the different tastes and how they blend together. This can help you notice the different qualities of the food. The experience is a little like you are listening to the different instruments that make up a symphony or like looking at both the forest and the individual trees.

If you are eating something new with a new name, say that name to yourself several times so you can remember it. Then, as you pay attention to the tastes, say that name again and again to yourself, so you make the connection. Later, you may be able to recreate the taste experience you had by saying the name again.

Eat slowly and focus your attention on what you are eating. Savor the food, and take your time doing so. If you are eating with others, try not to talk as you savor each dish to avoid distracting your attention from this process. Perhaps work out an agreement with your dining partners in advance, so that you can participate in this activity together and compare your experiences later.

With your attention focused on what you are eating, you might think of some of the following to help attune your awareness:

- Notice how the food on your plate is arranged. Consider the composition or balance of what you see before you, and notice if you have any impressions or associations with what you see. For instance, if you are looking at some meat, you may experience a feeling of strength and power. If you are looking at some vegetables, you might feel a sense of lightness and delicacy. Other foods may have a feeling of softness and warmth.

- Then look at the colors of the foods before you. Observe the relationship of the colors to each other, as if you are an artist or viewer contemplating a painting. Let any impressions and thoughts come to you. Be receptive to whatever this plate or display of food suggests.

- Pay attention to any smells as you look. Try closing your eyes. The smells may become more intense, for you have shut off your visual sense, and are concentrating on your sense of smell. Try to focus on individual smells and see if you can pick them out. If you can pick out these individual smells, shift your attention from smell to smell. Then go back and forth from these to the overall smell.

- Imagine how the food might taste, based on how the food looks or smells to you. If the food is already familiar, imagine that you are tasting it now. If it is unfamiliar, imagine yourself tasting it and experience what you think it might be like.

Begin eating the food. Keep your eyes open or closed as you prefer, or perhaps alternate and notice the differences. Allow plenty of time as you take each bite to pay attention to what you experience.

Notice your immediate impression of the taste. How might you describe this? Is it sweet? Sour? Strong? Mild? Rich? Use any adjectives you can think of to describe to yourself what you are tasting.

Notice if you have any feelings, images, memories, or other reactions evoked by the food. Perhaps it reminds you of a time when you ate similar food before, or maybe you suddenly see some vivid mind-pictures or symbols.

Tuning Into Your Environment

Second, tune in to the ambience of your environment to add to your eating experience, especially while waiting for your food to be served.

Start by looking around. Notice the decor, the type of clientele, the style of the menu. Think about how these things fit together. Do they create a feeling of synthesis or unity for you, a sense that everything matches? Or does anything feel strange, jarring, or out of place? For instance, some eating places have a quality of total elegance, from the styling of the interior, to the dress and manner of the waiters, to the fancy type on the menu. Other restaurants may have a simple, down-to-earth feeling. Notice if the clientele fit in with the overall ambience. They may be dressed very well in a place that is elegant, whereas in a more homey type of place, they may be dressed more casually or like they stopped on their way to work.

Besides looking, bring your senses into play. Pay attention to the sounds you hear. Create a soundscape of your environment as you listen. Notice the smells around you. Perhaps create a patchwork quilt of smells.

Focus your attention on the other patrons. Imagine who they might be, what they might be saying to each other, what they might be feeling.

If you have been in other restaurants in this area, think about how the environment differs here from these other places. Notice your reactions and feelings about these differences. Frequently, you will find your experience is quite different, and as you think about it, you'll notice more of these differences. The details and textures will fill in as you concentrate.

Noticing Any Cultural and Regional Differences

Third, if you are traveling to a new place, notice any cultural and regional differences in the way the food is prepared and served, in the ingredients used, and in how it tastes. In addition, notice how these cultural and regional differences reflect that particular society.

For example, in Japanese restaurants, you will notice an aesthetic delicacy about the way the food is prepared and presented. It looks like a work of art, as each piece of food is carefully shaped and balanced. This reflects a similar aesthetic you may notice in Japanese society, such as in the soft flowing and balanced lines of Japanese art and in the quiet beauty of Japanese gardens and architecture.

By contrast, in Russian restaurants, you may find the food has an earthy heaviness, reflecting a down-to-earth and serious quality in other aspects of Russian life, such as in its architecture and in its realistic, thoughtful style of painting.

In restaurants of other cultures and different regions of the U.S., you'll notice other patterns and themes.

So start looking, and besides enjoying the food, notice how it reflects a way of life. Think about how it reflects the personality of the culture or place it comes from. And as you pay attention, you'll become more in touch with that culture.

Other Books by the Author

Here are other books on achieving success or improving work relationships by the author:

- *WANT IT, SEE IT, GET IT! VISUALIZE YOUR WAY TO SUCCESS*

- *MIND POWER: PICTURE YOUR WAY TO SUCCESS*

- *THE EMPOWERED MIND: HOW TO HARNESS THE CREATIVE FORCE WITHIN YOU*

- *THE INNOVATIVE EDGE*

- *17 TOP SECRETS FOR HOW TO KEEP YOUR JOB OR FIND NEW WORK TODAY*

- *30 DAYS TO A MORE POWERFUL MEMORY*

- *ENJOY: 101 LITTLE THINGS TO ADD FUN TO YOUR WORK EVERYDAY*

- *DISAGREEMENTS, DISPUTES, AND ALL-OUT WAR*

- *A SURVIVAL GUIDE FOR WORKING WITH HUMANS*

- *A SURVIVAL GUIDE FOR WORKING WITH BAD BOSSES*

- *A SURVIVAL GUIDE TO MANAGING EMPLOYEES FROM HELL*

- *LET'S HAVE A SALES PARTY*

- *SUCCESS IN MLM, NETWORK MARKETING, AND PERSONAL SELLING*

- *HOW TO COLLECT THE MONEY PEOPLE OWE YOU*

Author Contact Information

Here's how to contact the author for information about other books and about speaking for your organization or putting on workshops and seminars for your organization:

> Gini Graham Scott, Ph.D.
> Director
> Changemakers
> 6114 La Salle, #358
> Oakland, CA 94611
> (510) 339-1625 ; Fax : (510) 339-1626
> changemakers@pacbell.net
> www.ginigrahamscott.com

Or visit Gini Graham Scott's Websites for her books:

> www.wantitseeitgetit.com (featuring *Want It, See It, Get It!*)
> www.enjoythebook.com *(featuring Enjoy! 101 Little Ways to Add Fun to Your Work Everyday)*

> www.workwithgini.com (books on improving work relationships)

> www.findworkwithgini.com (featuring *17 Top Secrets for How to Keep Your Job or Find New Work Today)*

www.workingwithhumans.com (featuring *A Survival Guide for Working with Humans, A Survival Guide to Managing Employees from Hell,* and *Disagreements, Disputes, and All-Out War)*

www.badbosses.net (featuring *A Survival Guide for Working with Bad Bosses)*